A Scots Kist

D0317169

Oliver & Boyd

in association with The Burns Federation

COVER   *Pitlessie Fair* (detail) by David Wilkie, reproduced by permission of the National Gallery of Scotland.

Kist *n.* Also *kest*; *kyist, kjist* (She); *cust*, and dim. *kistie, -y.* A chest, box, coffer, esp. a (farm-) servant's trunk; a treasury. Also a chestful.

Acknowledgements

The publishers are grateful to the following for permission to reproduce copyright material:

Aberdeen University Press for 'There's a Fairmer that I ken o'' and 'Fut like Folk' by J. C. Milne; J. K. Annand for 'Holidays', 'Conductress' and 'Crocodile'; Calder & Boyars (Publishers) Ltd. for Act IV of 'Jamie the Saxt' by Robert McLellan; Faber & Faber Ltd. for 'Wee Jock Todd' from *Sun and Candlelight* and 'The Fox's Skin' from *The Turn of the Day* by Marion Angus and for 'The Image of God' by Joe Corrie; Robert Garioch for 'Embro to the Ploy'; T. T. Kilbucho (Tam Todd) for 'The Cobbler' and 'Daith an' the Gang'ril'; Hugh MacDiarmid for 'Crowdieknowe' and 'The Eemis Stane'; Stephen Mulrine for 'The Coming of the Wee Malkies'; The Estate of the late Dr Neil Munro and William Blackwood & Sons Ltd. for 'Wee Teeny' by Neil Munro; John Murray (Publishers) Ltd. for 'Price' from *Bonnie Joann* and 'The Rowan' from *Northern Lights* by Violet Jacob; The Trustees of the National Library of Scotland for 'The Gowk' by William Soutar; The Editor of *Punch* for 'Glen, a sheepdog' by Milton Brown and 'Poaching in Excelsis' by G. K. Menzies; Mrs Alice Mitchell for 'The Auld Doctor', 'The Pawkie Duke' and 'The Lum Hat Wantin' the Croon' by Dr David Rorie.

While every effort has been made to trace copyright owners, apologies are made for any omissions in the above list.

Oliver & Boyd
Robert Stevenson House
1–3 Baxter's Place
Leith Walk, Edinburgh EH1 3AF
A Division of Longman Group Limited

ISBN 0 05 003309 3

First published 1972
This selection published 1979
Reprinted 1979
Printed in Great Britain by Spottiswoode
Ballantyne Limited, Colchester and London

Contents

Introduction

One of the most heartening aspects of post-war Scottish culture has been the change in the way it is regarded by Scottish cultural and educational institutions. Within even the last fifteen years one can see dramatic and concrete evidence that a new importance is being set on the preservation and development of our national traditions in literature, the visual arts, in music and song. The Scottish Arts Council gives generous amounts of money to Scottish creative artists; the Universities now teach courses in Scottish history and literature; numerous new and effective societies, from the Association for Scottish Literary Studies to the Scots Language Society, from the Saltire Society to the Universities Committee on Scottish Literature, have been actively recording, publishing and generally disseminating the Scottish Heritage.

In this cultural revival the importance of the Scots language has been a major, sometimes controversial, topic. How large should it loom in our schools? Should Scots be allowed to survive in a modern European context? Ever since Hugh MacDiarmid's great lyrics, the answer to both questions has been a positive one, sounding increasingly clear—till, in the Scottish Education Department's 1976 publication *Scottish Literature in the Secondary School* (which had the blessing and encouragement of the Scottish Central Committee on English in schools), Jack Aitken finished an excellent discussion of the topic by saying that

> our pupils deserve the chance to learn as much as we can offer them about their own language in their own environment, about its history and its present condition and their own position in this, at the same time acquiring tolerance for the language of their fellow-countrymen and some degree of security in speech for themselves. This would seem to call for much more talk and writing of and about Scots in our schools.

Alexander MacMillan's 1972 selection for the Burns Federation's anthology *The New Scots Reader* anticipated this call. Indeed, the publishers may take some pride in being pioneers in the field, since *The New Scots Reader* developed from the original three *Scots Readers* of Thomas Henderson and J. C. Smith. MacMillan's basis of selection was wise; he took the poems and passages which had proved most popular in the Burns Federation School Competitions, thus tapping a source of vitality that fills this collection. There are some of the great, stark Ballads, going centuries back in oral tradition; there are Ballads of the supernatural and songs of simple, comic and earthy matters. Yet, while the emphasis is always on the richness of the spoken language, with music never very far off, the selection pays due attention to our great poets from Burns to MacDiarmid, and our great novelists and dramatists, from Galt to Robert McLellan.

This new edition, *A Scots Kist*, is based on *The New Scots Reader*. It retains all the most popular pieces from the parent anthology, and also takes the opportunity to add some poems in keeping with today's tastes. One of the things about these *Scots Readers* which I particularly like is the way in which they have evolved. Behind their conception lies a willingness to alter, to adjust according to changing society. Thus this selection has moved, I believe, in the right direction, from the representation of an older, pastoral and perhaps 'kailyard' Scotland in the direction of the more complex, industrialised and restless Scotland of today. I welcome the new poems by MacDiarmid, Soutar and Mulrine, and hope that *A Scots Kist* may long continue its lively and changing career, reflecting more and more of our modern as well as our traditional Scottish writers of Scots. Scottish poetry and drama continue to thrive, and the *Kist* plays an important part in their encouragement.

Finally, it should be stressed that *A Scots Kist* is not only a lively and indispensable teaching text. Anyone who comes to it looking for an amusing, diverse, colourful treasurehouse of living Scottish poetry and prose will be more than satisfied with its achievement. It is to my mind the least costly, least pretentious and most successful anthology of literature in Scots on the market.

Douglas Gifford
(Lecturer in Scottish Literature, Department of English Studies, University of Strathclyde)

Tam o' the Linn

Tam o' the Linn cam' up the gait,[1]　　　　　　[1]road, way
Wi' twenty puddins on a plate,
And every puddin' had a pin—
'There's wud eneuch here,' quo' Tam o' the Linn.

Tam o' the Linn had nae breeks to wear,
He coft[2] him a sheep's-skin to mak' him a pair,　　[2]bought
The fleshy side oot, the woolly side in—
'It's fine summer cleidin','[3] quo' Tam o' the Linn.　[3]clothing

Tam o' the Linn and a' his bairns,
They fell in the fire in ilk ither's airms;
'Oh,' quo' the bunemost,[4] 'I hae a het skin'—　　[4]the one on
'It's hetter below,' quo' Tam o' the Linn.　　　　top

Tam o' the Linn gaed to the moss
To seek a stable to his horse;
The moss was open, and Tam fell in—
'I've stabled mysel',' quo' Tam o' the Linn.

　　　　　　　　　　　　　　　　Anon

Whistle, Whistle, Auld Wife

'Whistle, whistle, auld wife,
　　An' ye'se get a hen.'
'I wadna whistle,' quo' the wife,
　　'Though ye wad gie me ten.'

'Whistle, whistle, auld wife,
　　An' ye'se get a cock.'
'I wadna whistle,' quo' the wife,
　　'Though ye'd gie me a flock.'

'Whistle, whistle, auld wife,
　　An' ye'se get a goun.'
'I wadna whistle,' quo' the wife,
　　'For the best ane i' the town.'

'Whistle, whistle, auld wife,
    An' ye'se get a coo.'
'I wadna whistle,' quo' the wife,
    'Though ye wad gie me two.'

'Whistle, whistle, auld wife,
    An' ye'se get a man.'
'Wheeple-whauple,' quo' the wife,
    'I'll whistle gin I can.'

                                    Anon

Willie Winkie

Wee Willie Winkie rins through the toun,
Up stairs and doun stairs in his nicht-gown,
¹rattling Tirling¹ at the window, crying at the lock,
'Are the weans in their bed, for it's now ten
    o'clock?'

'Hey, Willie Winkie, are ye coming ben?
The cat's singing grey thrums to the sleeping hen,
²sprawled The dog's spelder'd² on the floor, and disna gie a
    cheep,
But here's a waukrife laddie that winna fa' asleep.'

Onything but sleep, you rogue! glow'ring like the
    moon;
Rattling in an airn jug wi' an airn spoon,
Rumbling, tumbling round about, crawing like a
    cock,
Skirling like a kenna-what, wauk'ning sleeping
    folk.

'Hey, Willie Winkie—the wean's in a creel!
Wamblin' aff a body's knee like a very eel,
Ruggin' at the cat's lug, and rav'llin' a' her
    thrums—
Hey, Willie Winkie—see, there he comes!'

2

Wearied is the mither that has a stoorie[3] wean,   ^{[3]restless}
A wee stumpie stousie,[4] that canna rin his lane.   [4]sturdy little
That has a battle aye wi' sleep before he'll close an   fellow
    e'e—
But a kiss frae aff his rosy lips gies strength anew to
    me.

William Miller

The Sair Finger

You've hurt your finger? Puir wee man!
    Your pinkie?[1] Deary me!   [1]little finger
Noo, juist you haud it that wey till
    I get my specs and see!

My, so it is—and there's the skelf![2]   [2]splinter
    Noo, dinna greet nae mair.
See there—my needle's gotten't out!
    I'm sure that wasna sair?

And noo, to make it hale the morn,
    Put on a wee bit saw,[3]   [3]salve
And tie a bonnie hankie roun't—
    Noo, there na—rin awa'!

Your finger sair ana'? Ye rogue,
    Ye're only lettin' on.
Weel, weel, then—see noo, there ye are,
    Row'd up the same as John!

Walter Wingate

The Marriage of Robin Redbreast and the Wren

There was an auld gray Poussie Baudrons and she gaed awa' down by a water-side, and there she saw a wee Robin Redbreast happin' on a brier; and Poussie Baudrons says: 'Where's tu gaun, wee Robin?' And wee Robin says: 'I'm gaun awa' to the king to sing him a sang this guid Yule morning.' And Poussie Baudrons says: 'Come here, wee Robin, and I'll let you see a bonny white ring round my neck.' But wee Robin says: 'Na, na! gray Poussie Baudrons; na, na! Ye worry't the wee mousie; but ye'se no worry me.' So see Robin flew awa' till he came to a fail[1] fauld-dike, and there he saw a gray greedy gled[2] sitting. And gray greedy gled says: 'Where's tu gaun, wee Robin?' And wee Robin says: 'I'm gaun awa' to the king to sing him a sang this guid Yule morning.' And gray greedy gled says: 'Come here, wee Robin, and I'll let ye see a bonny feather in my wing.' But wee Robin says: 'Na, na! gray greedy gled; na, na! ye pookit[3] a' the wee lintie; but ye'se no pook me.' So wee Robin flew awa' till he came to the cleuch[4] o' a craig, and there he saw slee Tod Lowrie[5] sitting. And slee Tod Lowrie says: 'Where's tu gaun, wee Robin?' And wee Robin says: 'I'm gaun awa' to the king to sing him a sang this guid Yule morning.' And slee Tod Lowrie says: 'Come here, wee Robin, and I'll let ye see a bonny spot on the tap o' my tail.' But wee Robin says: 'Na, na! slee Tod Lowrie; na, na! Ye worry't the wee lammie; but ye'se no worry me.' So wee Robin flew awa' till he came to a bonny burnside, and there he saw a wee callant sitting. And the wee callant says: 'Where's tu gaun, wee Robin?' And wee Robin says: 'I'm gaun awa' to the king to sing him a sang this guid Yule morning.' And the wee callant says: 'Come here, wee Robin, and I'll gie ye a wheen grand moolins[6] out o' my pooch.' But wee Robin says: 'Na, na! wee callant; na, na! Ye speldert[7] the

[1]turf	[2]kite hawk	[3]plucked
[4]hollow	[5]the sly fox	[6]crumbs
[7]cut up		

4

gowdspink; but ye'se no spelder me.' So wee Robin flew awa' till he came to the king, and there he sat on a winnock sole[8] and sang the king a bonny sang. And the king says to the queen: 'What'll we gie to wee Robin for singing us this bonny sang?' And the queen says to the king: 'I think we'll gie him the wee wran to be his wife.' So wee Robin and the wee wran were married, and the king and the queen and a' the court danced at the waddin'; syne he flew awa' hame to his ain water-side and happit on a brier.

Robert Burns's Version

[8]window-sill

The Horny Gollach

The horny gollach's an awesome beast,
  Souple an' scaley;
He has twa horns an' a hantle o' feet
  An' a forky tailie.

Anon

Bonnie George Campbell

Hie upon Hielands,
  and laigh upon Tay,
Bonnie George Campbell
  rode out on a day.

He saddled, he bridled,
  and gallant rode he,
And hame cam his guid horse,
  but never cam he.

Out cam his mother dear,
  greeting fu sair,
And out cam his bonnie bryde,
  riving her hair.

'The meadow lies green,
  the corn is unshorn,
But bonnie George Campbell
  will never return.'

Saddled and bridled
  and booted rode he,
A plume in his helmet,
  A sword at his knee.

But toom cam his saddle,
  all bloody to see,
Oh, hame cam his guid horse,
  but never cam he!

Anon

Wee Jock Todd

The King cam' drivin' through the toon,
Slae and stately through the toon;
He bo'ed tae left, he bo'ed tae richt,
An' we bo'ed back as weel we micht;
But wee Jock Todd he couldna bide,
He was daft tae be doon at the waterside;
Sae he up an' waved his fishin' rod—
        Och, wee Jock Todd!

But in the quaiet hoor o' dreams,
The lang street streekit wi' pale moonbeams,
Wee Jock Todd cam' ridin' doon,
Slae an' solemn through the toon.
He bo'ed tae left, he bo'ed tae richt
(It maun ha'e been a bonnie sicht)
An' the King cam' runnin'—he couldna bide—
He was mad tae be doon at the waterside;
Sae he up wi' his rod and gaed a nod
        Tae wee Jock Todd.

Marion Angus

Schule in June

There's no a clood in the sky,
 The hill's clear as can be,
An' the broon road's windin' ower it,
 But—no for me!

It's June, wi' a splairge¹ o' colour   ¹splash
 In glen an' on hill,
An' its' me wad be lyin' up yonner,
 But then—there's the schule.

There's a wude wi' a burn rinnin' through it,
 Caller an' cool,
Whaur the sun splashes licht on the bracken
 An' dapples the pool.

There's a sang in the soon' o' the watter,
 Sang sighs in the air,
An' the worl' disnae maitter a docken
 To yin that's up there.

A hop an' a step frae the windie,
 Just fower mile awa',
An' I could be lyin' there thinkin'
 O' naething ava'.

Ay!—the schule is a winnerfu' place,
 Gin ye tak it a' roon,
An' I've nae objection to lessons
 Whiles—but in June?

                                        Robert Bain

The Sunday School Soirée

'It's an awfu' peety ye canna get in to the surree,' re-marked Willie Thomson to his chum, who was accompanying him to the church hall wherein an entertainment to the Sunday school children was about to be held.

Macgregor looked exceedingly gloomy.

'If ye hadna plunkit[1] sae mony times, ye wud ha'e gotten a ticket; but ye wis absent ower often,' continued Willie, without meaning to be offensive.

'Ye wud ha'e plunkit yersel' whiles, if ye hadna been feart,' retorted Macgregor.

'I wudna!'

'Ay, wud ye! An' it's jist as bad as plunkin' to spend yer bawbee on sweeties an' let on ye've pit it in the heathen mishnary boax.'

'When did I dae that?' Willie loudly demanded, without meeting the other's eye.

'Fine ye ken when ye done it.'

'Weel, if I ever done it, I aye gi'ed ye hauf the sweeties.'

'So ye did, Wullie,' said Macgregor more kindly. 'But ye needna think ye deserve to get in to the surree ony mair nor me. D'ye hear?'

'Ay, I hear,' Willie replied with some irritation in his voice. 'But ye sudna ha'e plunkit sae often, fur ye micht ha'e kent ye wudna get a ticket—'

'If ye say that again, I'll – I'll—'

'I'll no' say it again.'

'Weel, that's a' richt. But it wisna fair to ha'e the surree sae early this year. It's faur earlier nor last year. If I had kent it wis to be sae early I wudna ha'e plunkit till efter the surree wis ower.'

'But this is an extra surree. It's the new meenister that's peyin' fur't.'

'Weel, it's no' fair coontin' merks fur an extra surree. An' I dinna think it'll be a vera nice yin. Ye'll get naethin' efter the tea but twa-three hymns an' a lang lectur.'

[1] played truant

8

'We're to get a maygic lantern an' a con*joo*rer,' said Willie elatedly.

'Are ye?' said Macgregor, taken aback. 'He maun be a nice meenister. But it wisna fair coontin' merks fur an extra surree. . . . I wisht I hadna plunkit sae often.'

'I wisht ye hadna,' the other sympathetically returned. The twain walked a score of yards in silence.

'D'ye think I can jink the man at the door?' enquired Macgregor suddenly.

'It's aye the beadle that tak's the tickets at the surrees,' his friend replied.

'Aw! He's ower fly,' said Macgregor dolefully, 'I doot I canna jink him. If it wis yin o' the teachers, I wud try it.'

'Ye best no' try it wi' the beadle. I – I doot ye canna get in, Macgreegor,' said Willie hopelessly.

Macgregor considered. 'Can ye no' tak' a fit on the doorstep?' he asked at last, 'I yinst seen a lot o' folk getting inside a show fur naethin' when a wife tuk a fit just at the door.'

Willie shook his head. 'I dinna ken hoo to tak' a fit; an' if I wis takin' yin, they maybe wudna let me in to the surree.'

'I didna think o' that, Wullie. . . . Wud it no' dae to say I had lost ma ticket?'

'Naw! They wud speir yer name, an' then luk up the book to see if ye had the richt merks. They're awfu' fly at oor Sawbath schule. Ye sudna ha'e plunkit sae mony—'

'If ye say that again, I'll—'

'I didna mean to say it, Macgreegor.'

'Weel, dinna say it! . . . I wudna strike ye, onywey, Ye're ower peely-wally.'

'I'm no'!'

'Ay, are ye! . . . But ha'e *you* got the richt merks in the book?' enquired Macgregor abruptly.

'Ay,' returned Willie proudly.

'But I bet ye a thoosan' pound ye wudna get in if ye had lost yer ticket.'

'I wud get in fine,' said the virtuous William.

'Weel, ye can just dae't! Gi'e's yer ticket!' cried Macgregor.

His friend regarded him blankly.

'Come on! Gi'e's yer ticket,' Macgregor repeated pleasantly, 'I'll gi'e ye ma next Setturday penny, if ye'll promise to gi'e us hauf whit ye buy wi' 't.'

Still the other looked woefully undecided. They had now almost reached the door of the hall.

'Ma next Setturday penny,' said Macgregor again, 'Come on, Wullie.'

Willie, who got no regular Saturday penny, was certainly tempted by the proposal; but after a brief period of consideration he said, 'Naw,' and quickened his steps.

Whereupon Macgregor exclaimed, 'I'm no' in wi' ye ony mair,' and turned away.

This was too much for Willie. He turned also, and hastened after Macgregor, crying: 'I'll gi'e ye the ticket, I'll gi'e ye the ticket!'

'Wull ye?' said his friend, halting.

'Ay. But – but I'll no' try to get in to the surree.'

'Whit?'

'I'll let ye gang in instead o' me.'

'Nae fears! I wudna dae that, Wullie. No' likely!'

'Wud ye no' gang in wi'oot me?'

'Awa' an' bile yer heid! As if I wud gang in wi'oot ye! Jist you gi'e me the ticket an' come to the door efter me, an' I'll shin get ye in. An' if they'll no' let ye in. I'll gi'e ye back yer ticket, an' I'll gang awa' home.'

The ticket being transferred, they approached the entrance to the hall of happiness.

'Wullie,' said Macgregor in a whisper, 'can ye no' greet?'

'Whit wey?'

'To mak' the beadle vexed fur ye because ye've lost yer ticket. Ye see? . . . Try an' greet, Wullie.'

'I canna,' said Willie despairingly, 'I'm ower big to greet.'

'Weel, try an' luk awfu' meeserable.'

Willie succeeded in doing so, and they climbed the few steps to the doorway, where the church officer had taken his stand.

Macgregor held out the ticket, and carelessly pointing to his friend, who looked like running away, remarked:

'This yin's lost his ticket.'

'Eh?' said the beadle.

'I'm sayin' he's lost his ticket.'

'Whaur did he loss it?'

'Ootbye.'

'Mphm. He's no' the first yin that's lost his ticket the nicht,' the beadle observed severely, 'What's yer name?' he demanded of Willie.

'Wullie Thomson.'

'Wha's yer teacher?'

'Maister M'Culloch.'

The beadle passed in several children who presented their tickets, and then, opening the swing-doors, bawled across the hall: 'Maister M'Culloch, ye're wantit, please.'

'I'll wait fur ye inside, Wullie,' hurriedly whispered Macgregor, afraid of meeting the young man who was his teacher as well as Willie's.

'But – but if he winna let me in,' said Willie.

'If he winna let ye in, I'll come oot again. Ye needna be feart, Wullie.'' And Macgregor disappeared through the swing-doors.

Two minutes later he was joined by his chum.

'I kent ye wud get in,' said Macgregor.

'Ay,' said Willie, adding, 'but *you*'re nickit,[2] Macgreegor.'

'Did he see me?'

'Ay; he seen ye!'

'Is he gaun to pit me oot?'

'I dinna ken. He jist askit me whit wey ye didna wait ootside fur me. But he wis rale nice. He wisna angry at me fur gi'ein' – I mean, fur lossin' – ma ticket.'

'Wis he no'? Come awa' this wey, Wullie. I'm no' wantin' him to catch me.'

'Maybe he wudna pit ye oot,' said Willie, following his friend, 'He's rale kind. D'ye mind when ye fell in the glaur,[3] an' he cleaned yer face wi' his guid hanky?'

'Ay. But I'm no' wanting' him to speak to me the nicht. We'll get a sate at the back thonder.'

'But we'll no' see the magic lantern an' the con*joo*rer as weel there,' the other objected.

[2]caught   [3]mud

'We'll gang furrit when they screw doon the lichts fur the lantern. Come on! There a man gi'ein' oot the pokes, an' thonder anither comin' wi' the tea.'

'Haud yer tongue,' said a little girl beside them: 'the meenister's gaun to ask a blessin'.'

'Aw, *you*'re here, Maggie, are ye?' retorted Macgregor as jauntily as possible, recognising a dweller in his own street, who usually saluted him by putting out her tongue.

'Ay, it's jist me. Hoo did ye get in, Macgreegor?' she enquired, immediately the brief grace was finished.

'Through the door,' replied Macgregor smartly.

'An' ye'll gang oot through the door gey shin,' Maggie exclaimed unkindly, 'I ken fine ye had nae ticket. Ye're jist a cheat! An' cheatery'll choke ye!'

Fortunately most of the youngsters were already being served with tea and bags of buns, otherwise more heads would have turned in Macgregor's direction.

'If ye wisna a lassie, I wud knock the face aff ye!' the boy muttered wildly. 'I'm no' a cheat!'

'I ken ye're no' a cheat, Macgreegor,' said the small voice of another little girl.

'Ye dinna ken him, Katie,' said Maggie sharply.

'Ay; I ken him. He wudna be a cheat,' returned Katie gently, with a shy glance at her hero.

But Willie was dragging his friend away to another part of the hall, and the latter took no notice of his girl champion.

Twenty minutes later Willie genially observed: 'I've ett mair nor you, Macgreegor.'

'Ye've a bigger mooth,' returned Macgregor sulkily. He felt that nearly everyone was watching him, and Maggie's words rankled.

After tea the minister delivered a very brief address on Honesty and Truth, and the youngster was glad when the speaker finished. Then came the conjurer, but it was not until the lights were lowered for the magic lantern item of the entertainment that Macgregor began to feel free to take his pleasure with the other children.

'We'll gang furrit noo,' he whispered to Willie, and in the dim light the twain crept forward and crushed themselves into a seat well in front, much to the indignation of its occupants.

'If ye kick me again,' said Macgregor, hoarsely, to the boy next him, 'I'll gi'e ye a shot on the nose!'

'Keep quiet, Macgregor,' said a voice from the bench behind, and the voice was that of Mr M'Culloch, his teacher.

Macgregor kept *very* quiet throughout the lantern exhibition.

As the children departed from the hall, each received a bag of sweets and shook hands with the minister and also with his or her teacher.

For a moment Macgregor was tempted to make a bolt for freedom, but his courage prevailed, and, after receiving his sweets, he kept his place in the line of boys and girls that filed slowly towards the door. And–strange thing!– he received as kindly a look and handshake from the minister as did any of the other scholars. So surprised was he that he dropped the sweets, and lost his place in the line, having to stand aside till all had passed. And then he found himself shaking hands with the minister a second time.

A nasty choky feeling came in his throat as he approached his teacher.

'Well, Macgregor,' said Mr M'Culloch ever so kindly, laying a light hand on the boy's shoulder.

Macgregor gave a queer, gulping sound. 'I'm no' wantin' the sweeties!' he cried, and, shoving the bag into the teacher's hand, he rushed from the hall.

Willie was waiting for him in the street. 'Did ye catch it frae Maister M'Culloch?' he enquired.

'Naw,' said Macgregor sharply.

They walked some distance in silence, Willie observing that his chum was in trouble.

But at last Willie said in a shamed manner: 'I – I think I'll no' buy sweeties again wi' ma heathen mishnary boax bawbee.'

There was another long silence, broken again by Willie.

'Are ye gaun to the schule next Sawbath?' he asked timidly.

'I'll see.'

This was not encouraging, so Willie changed the subject.

'They're awfu' guid sweeties we got the nicht,' remarked Willie, conveying a couple from his pocket to his mouth.

'Ay,' assented Macgregor dismally, and turned abruptly away.

He walked slowly home, and when he reached the house his father was waiting for him at the door.

'Ye furgot yer sweeties at the surree, Macgreegor.'

'Eh?' cried the boy, taken aback.

'Yer teacher wis here the noo an' left thur fur ye. He didna want ye to be disappintit. Ye're the lucky yin!' said his father, laughing and bringing *two* bags from behind his back.

His son smiled broadly, it might even have been virtuously.

From *Wee Macgreegor Again*, by J. J. Bell

The Tod

'Eh.' quo' the tod, 'it's a braw licht nicht,
The win's i' the wast, an' the mune shines bricht,
The win's i' the wast, an' the mune shines bricht,
    An' I'll awa' to the toun, O.

[1] stunted bushes

'I was doun amang yon shepherd's scroggs;[1]
I'd like to hae been worried by his dogs;
But by my sooth I minded his hoggs
    When I cam' to the toun, O.'

He's taen the gray goose by the green sleeve,
'Eh! ye auld witch, nae langer sall ye leeve;
Your flesh it is tender, your banes I maun prieve[2]
    For that I cam to the toun, O!'

[2] taste

Up gat the auld wife oot o' her bed,
An' oot o' the window she shot her head,
'Eh, gudeman! the gray goose is dead,
    An' the tod has been i' the toun, O!'

Anon

The Racing Pigeon

The doo smeekt[1] up intil the lift,
Frae Rennes-Ward it flew,
A siller-checkit, pink ee'd bird,
A hame-ward racin' doo'.

[1]went up
like smoke

Win hame, win hame, her hert said lood,
Win hame afore the nicht,
Gin ye sit on a clood an scart your heid,
Ye'll need the starnes licht.

The wind gied a gurry an blew gey strang,
Jaggit cloods duntit her sair,
An the sun keekit oot on the daft-like bird,
Cuttin wee holes in the air.

Syne doon faur doon she glimp'd the waves,
Castin their heids on hie,
But she focht on abune till the rain fell doon,
Near blint her roon-ringet ee.

Still faur frae hame, whan gloamin cam,
In a frichtenin' lan' o' mirk,
Forfochend[2] a' wee, she lichtit doon,
Pit her heid aneath her sark.

[2]near
exhaustion

An dreamt a dream o' ripe-stookit corn,
An a daunerin' burn near dry,
A saft feather bed amang the strae
An a gether o' freens ootbye.

Weel, did she win hame? Oh ah canna tell.
There's a lost doo' sits in that tree,
Comes speirin' doon at my feet as ah write —
An that's guid eneugh for me.

                              Sandy Thomas Ross

Holidays

¹pouring out

²claimed
³linked arms

As I gang up the Castlehill
The bairns are skailin¹ frae the schule.
Some look neat and some look tykes,
Some on fute and some on bikes,
Some are trystit² by their mithers,
Ithers cleekit³ wi their brithers,
Some hae bags and some hae cases
But aa hae smiles upon their faces
For noo the holidays begin
And lessons for a while are dune.
It's nocht but fun and games aa day,
Nae mair wark, but lots o play
Until neist year the schule-bell caas
Them back to the maister and his tawse.

J. K. Annand

Conductress

When I growe up and leave the schule
I winna work in onie mill
But stick to my ambition still
And be a bus conductress.

Twa inside,
Fower up the stair.
That'll dae noo,
I daurna tak mair.
Haud on ticht.
Ring-ting-ting.
Move up the bus.
That's the very thing.
Thripence to the circus,
Fowerpence to the zoo,
Hae your fares ready
And I'll thank you.

J. K. Annand

Crocodile

When doukin[1] in the River Nile   [1]splashing
I met a muckle crocodile.   about
He flicked his tail, he blinked his ee,
Syne bared his ugsome teeth at me.

Says I, 'I never saw the like.
Cleaning your teeth maun be a fyke!
What sort a besom do ye hae
To brush a set o teeth like thae?'

The crocodile said, 'Nane ava.
I never brush my teeth at aa!
A wee bird redds them up, ye see,
And saves me monie a dentist's fee.'

                          J. K. Annand

The Piper o' Dundee

And wasna he a roguey,
A roguey, a roguey,
And wasna he a roguey,
The piper o' Dundee?

The piper came to our town,
To our town, to our town,
The piper came to our town,
And he played bonnilie.
He played a spring the laird to please,
A spring brent new[1] frae yont the seas;   [1]brand-new
And then he ga'e his bags a heeze,   dance
And played anither key.

He played *The Welcome owre the main*,
And *Ye'se be fou and I'se be fain*,
And *Auld Stuart's back again*,
Wi' muckle mirth and glee.
He played *The Kirk*, he played *The Quier*,
The *Mullin Dhu* and *Chevalier*,
And *Lang Awa'*, *but Welcome Here*,
Sae sweet, sae bonnilie.

It's some gat swords, and some gat nane,
And some were dancing mad their lane,
And mony a vow o' weir was ta'en,
That night at Amulrie!
There was Tullibardine and Burleigh,
And Struan, Keith, and Ogilvie,
And brave Carnegie, wha but he,
The piper o' Dundee?

Anon

The Lum Hat Wantin' the Croon

¹flood   The burn was big wi' spate,¹
An' there cam' tumlin' doon
²head over Tapsalteerie² the half o' a gate,
heels   Wi' an auld fish-hake an' a great muckle skate,
³tall hat An' a lum hat³ wantin' the croon.

The auld wife stude on the bank,
As they gaed swirling' roun',
She took a gude look an' syne says she,
'There's food an' there's firin' gaun to the sea,
An' a lum hat wantin' the croon.'

Sae she gruppit the branch o' a saugh,
An' she kicket aff ane o' her shoon,
An' she stuck oot her fit—but it caught in the gate,
An' awa she went wi' the great muckle skate,
An' the lum hat wantin' the croon.

She floatit fu' mony a mile,
Past cottage an' village an' toon,
She'd an awfu' time astride o' the gate,
Though it seemed to gree fine wi' the great muckle
    skate,
An' the lum hat wantin' the croon.

A fisher was walkin' the deck,
By the licht o' his pipe an' the mune,
When he sees an auld body astride o' a gate,
Come bobbin' alang in the waves wi' a skate,
An' a lum hat wantin' the croon.

'There's a man overboord!' cries he,
'Ye leear!' says she, 'I'll droon;
A man on a boord? It's a wife on a gate
It's auld Mistress Mackintosh here wi' a skate,
An' a lum hat wantin' the croon.'

Was she nippit to death at the Pole?
Has India bakit her broon?
I canna tell that, but whatever her fate,
I'll wager ye'll find it was shared by a skate,
An' a lum hat wantin' the croon.

There's a moral attached to my sang.
On greed ye should aye gie a froon,
When ye think o' the wife that was lost for a gate,
An' auld fish-hake an' a great muckle skate,
An' a lum hat wantin' the croon.

                                Dr David Rorie

Letter IV of 'The Ayrshire Legatees'

John Galt's picture of London, 1820–21, as seen through the eyes of the Rev. Dr. Pringle, Mrs. Pringle and their son and daughter. The family had left their Ayrshire parish to visit London in order to claim a fortune which the Reverend had inherited. The Pringle family write to their friends in the Ayrshire parish recounting their experiences.

Mrs. Pringle to Miss Mally Glencairn

LONDON

My Dear Miss Mally

You must not expect no particulars from me of our journey; but as Rachel is writing all the calamities that befell us to Bell Todd, you will, no doubt, hear of them. But all is nothing to my losses. I bought from the first hand, Mr. Treddles the manufacturer, two pieces of muslin, at Glasgow, such a thing not being to be had on any reasonable terms here, where they get all their fine muslins from Glasgow and Paisley; and in the same bocks with them I packit a small crock of our ain excellent poudered butter, with a delap[1] cheese, for I was told that such commodities are not to be had genuine in London. I likewise had in it a pot of marmlet,[2] which Miss Jenny Macbride gave me at Glasgow, assuring me that it was not only dentice, but a curiosity among the English, and my best new bumbeseen goun[3] in peper.[4] Howsomever, in the nailing of the bocks, which I did carefully with my oun hands, one of the nails gaed in ajee,[5] and broke the pot of marmlet, which, by the jolting of the ship, ruined the muslin, rottened the peper round the goun, which the shivers cut into more than twenty great holes. Over and above all, the crock with the butter was, no one can tell how, crackit, and the pickle lecking[6] out, and mixing with

[1]Dunlop	[2]marmalade	[3]bombazine gown
[4]paper	[5]on the slant	[6]leaking

20

the seerip[7] of the marmlet, spoilt the cheese. In short, at the object I beheld, when the bocks was opened, I could have ta'en to the greeting; but I behaved with more composity on the occasion, than the doctor thought it was in the power of nature to do. Howsomever, till I get a new goun and other things, I am obliged to be a prisoner, and as the doctor does not like to go to the counting-house of the agents without me, I know not what is yet to be the consequence of our journey. But it would need to be something; for we pay four guineas and a half a-week for our dry lodgings, which is at a degree more than the doctor's whole stipend. As yet, for the cause of these misfortunes, I can give you no account of London, but there is, as everybody kens, little thrift in their house-keeping. We just buy our tea by the quarter a pound, and our loaf sugar, broken in a peper bag, by the pound, which would be a disgrace to a decent family in Scotland, and when we order dinner, we get no more than just serves, so that we have no cold meat if a stranger were coming by chance, which makes an unco bare house. The servan lasses I cannot abide; they dress better at their wark, than ever I did on an ordinaire week-day at the manse, and this very morning I saw madam, the kitchen lass, mounted on a pair of pattens, washing the plain stenes before the door; na, for that matter, a bare foot is not to be seen within the four walls of London, at the least I have na seen no such thing.

Tell Miss Nanny Eydent that I have seen none of the fashions as yet, but we are going to the burial of the auld king next week, and I'll write her a particular account how the leddies are dressed; but every body is in deep mourning. Howsomever I have seen but little, and that only in a manner from the window; but I could not miss the opportunity of a frank that Andrew has got, and he's waiting for the pen, you must escuse haste. From your sincere friend,

Janet Pringle

John Galt

[7] syrup

The Puddock

A Puddock sat by the lochan's brim,
An' he thocht there was never a puddock like him.
He sat on his hurdies, he waggled his legs,
¹[1]sedges An' cockit his heid as he glowered throu' the seggs.[1]
The bigsy wee cratur' was feeling that prood,
He gapit his mou' an' he croakit oot lood:
'Gin ye'd a' like tae see a richt puddock,' quo' he,
'Ye'll never, I'll sweer, get a better nor me.
I've fem'lies an' wives an' a weel-plenished hame,
Wi' drink for my thrapple an' meat for my wame.
The lasses aye thocht me a fine strappin' chiel,
An' I ken I'm a rale bonny singer as weel.
I'm nae gaun tae blaw, but th' truth I maun tell—
I believe I'm the verra MacPuddock himsel'.'

A heron was hungry an' needin' tae sup,
Sae he nabbit th' puddock and gollup't him up;
Syne runkled his feathers: 'A peer thing,' quo' he,
'But—puddocks is nae fat they eesed tae be.'

J. M. Caie

The Boy in the Train

Whit wey does the engine say *Toot-toot*?
  Is it feart to gang in the tunnel?
Whit wey is the furnace no pit oot
  When the rain gangs doon the funnel?
What'll I hae for my tea the nicht?
  A herrin', or maybe a haddie?
Has Gran'ma gotten electric licht?
  Is the next stop Kirkcaddy?

There's a hoodie-craw on yon turnip-raw!
   An' sea-gulls!—sax or seeven.
I'll no fa' oot o' the windae, Maw,
   It's sneckit, as sure as I'm leevin'.
We're into the tunnel! we're a' in the dark!
   But dinna be frichtit, Daddy,
We'll sune be comin' to Beveridge Park,
   And the next stop's Kirkcaddy!

Is yon the mune I see in the sky?
   It's awfu' wee an' curly.
See! there's a coo and a cauf ootbye,
   An' a lassie pu'in' a hurly!
He's chackit the tickets and gien them back,
   Sae gie me my ain yin, Daddy.
Lift doon the bag frae the luggage rack,
   For the next stop's Kirkcaddy!

There's a gey wheen boats at the harbour mou',
   And eh! dae ye see the cruisers?
The cinnamon drop I was sookin' the noo
   Has tummelt an' stuck tae ma troosers. . . .
I'll sune be ringin' ma Gran'ma's bell,
   She'll cry, 'Come ben, my laddie,'
For I ken mysel' by the queer-like smell
   That the next stop's Kirkcaddy!

                                        M.C.S.

The Fox's Skin

When the wark's a' dune and the world's a' still,
And whaups¹ are swoopin' across the hill,   ¹curlews
And mither stands cryin', 'Bairns, come ben,'
It's the time for the Hame o' the Pictish Men.

A sorrowfu' wind gaes up and doon,
An' me my lane in the licht o' the moon,
Gaitherin' a bunch o' the floorin' whin,
Wi' my auld fur collar hapt roond ma chin.

A star is shining on Morven Glen—
It shines on the Hame o' the Pictish Men.
Hither and yont their dust is blown.
But ane o' them's keekin' ahint yon stone.

His queer auld face is wrinkled and riven,
Like a raggedy leaf, sae drookit and driven.
There's nocht to be feared at his ancient ways,
For this is a' that iver he says:

'The same auld wind at its weary cry:
The blin'-faced moon in the misty sky;
A thoosand years o' clood and flame,
An' a' thing's the same an' aye the same—
The lass is the same in the fox's skin,
Gaitherin' the bloom o' the floorin' whin.'

Marion Angus

My Hoggie

What will I do gin my hoggie die?
    My joy, my pride, my hoggie!
My only beast, I had nae mae,
    And vow but I was vogie![1]

The lee-lang night we watch'd the fauld,
    Me and my faithfu' doggie;
We heard nought but the roaring linn,
    Amang the braes sae scroggie;

But the houlet cry'd frae the castle wa',
    The blitter[2] frae the boggie,
The tod reply'd upon the hill,
    I trembl'd for my hoggie.

When day did daw, and cocks did craw,
    The morning it was foggie;
An unco tyke lap o'er the dyke,
    And maist has kill'd my hoggie.

Robert Burns

[1] proud

[2] snipe

The Whistle

He cut a sappy sucker from the muckel rodden-
tree,[1]   [1]rowan
He trimmed it, an' he wet it, an' he thumped it on
his knee;
He never heard the teuchat[2] when the harrow   [2]lapwing
broke her eggs.
He missed the craggit[3] heron nabbin' puddocks in [3]long-
the seggs,   necked
He forgot to hound the collie at the cattle when
they strayed,
But you should hae seen the whistle that the wee
herd made!

He wheepled on't at mornin' an' he tweetled on't
at nicht,
He puffed his freckled cheeks until his nose sank
oot o' sicht,
The kye were late for milkin' when he piped them
up the closs,
The kitlins got his supper syne, an' he was beddit
boss;[4]   [4]empty
But he cared na doit[5] nor docken what they did or [5]fraction of
thocht or said,   a penny
There was comfort in the whistle that the wee herd
made.

For lyin' lang o' mornin's he had clawed the caup[6] [6]scraped
for weeks,   the bowl
But noo he had his bonnet on afore the lave had
breeks;
He was whistlin' to the porridge that were hott'rin'
on the fire,
He was whistlin' ower the travise[7] to the bailie in [7]partition
the byre;
Nae a blackbird nor a mavis, that hae pipin' for
their trade,
Was a marrow for the whistle that the wee herd
made.

25

He played a march to battle, it cam' dirlin' through
the mist,
Till the halflin' squared his shou'ders an' made
up his mind to 'list;
He tried a spring for wooers, though he wistna
what it meant,
But the kitchen-lass was lauchin' an' he thocht
she maybe kent;
He got ream an' buttered bannocks for the lovin'
lilt he played.
Wasna that a cheery whistle that the wee herd
made?

He blew them rants sae lively, schottisches, reels,
an' jigs,
The foalie flang his muckle legs an' capered owre
the rigs,
The grey-tailed futt'rat⁸ bobbit oot to hear his ain
strathspey,
The bawd⁹ cam' loupin' through the corn to 'Clean
Pease Strae';
The feet o' ilka man an' beast gat youkie¹⁰ when
he played—
Hae ye ever heard o' whistle like the wee herd
made?

But the snaw it stopped the herdin' an' the winter
brocht him dool,
When in spite o' hacks an' chilblains he was shod
again for school;
He couldna sough the catechis nor pipe the rule o'
three,
He was keepit in an' lickit when the ither loons got
free;
But he aften played the truant—'twas the only
thing he played,
For the maister brunt the whistle that the wee
herd made!

Charles Murray

26

The Comin' o' the Spring

There's no a muir in my ain land but's fu' o' sang
    the day,
Wi' the whaup, and the gowden plover, and the
    lintie upon the brae.
The birk in the glen is springin', the rowan-tree in
    the shaw,
And every burn is rinnin' wild wi' the meltin' o'
    the snaw.

The wee white cluds in the blue lift are hurryin'
    light and free,
Their shadows fleein' on the hills, where I, too,
    fain wad be;
The wind frae the west is blawing, and wi' it seems
    to bear
The scent o' the thyme and gowan thro' a' the
    caller air.

The herd doon the hillside's linkin'. O licht his
    heart may be
Whose step is on the heather, his glance ower muir
    and lea!
On the Moss are the wild ducks gatherin', whar
    the pules like diamonds lie,
And far up soar the wild geese, wi' weird unyirdly
    cry.

In mony a neuk the primrose lies hid frae stranger
    een,
An' the broom on the knowes is wavin' wi' its
    cludin'[1] o' gowd and green;   [1]clothing
Ower the first green sprigs o' heather the muir-
    fowl faulds his wing,
And there's nought but joy in my ain land at the
    comin' o' the Spring!

                     Lady John Scott

The Night's Rain

The thunder clap may clatter,
　The lichtnin' flare awa':
I'm listenin' to the water,
　And heed them nocht ava.

I canna think ò' sleepin':
　I canna hear eneuch,
The sang the trees are dreepin',
　The music o' the sheugh![1]

And 'neath the roof that's drummin
　Wi' mair than rhone[2] can kep,
Wi' faster fa' is comin'
　The plop upon the step.

My famished flowers are drinkin'
　In ilka drookit bed:
An' siller blabs are winkin'
　On ilka cabbage bled.

And in my blankets rowin'
　I think on hay an' corn—
I maist can hear them growin';
　We'll see an odds the morn.

Walter Wingate

[1] ditch

[2] roof-gutter

A Winter Night

When biting Boreas, fell and doure,[1]   [1]hard
Sharp shivers thro' the leafless bow'r;
When Phoebus gies a short-liv'd glow'r[2]   [2]stare
      Far south the lift,[3]   [3]sky
Dim-dark'ning through the flaky show'r,
      Or whirling drift:

Ae night the Storm the steeples rocked,
Poor Labour sweet in sleep was locked,
While burns, wi' snawy wreeths up-choked,
      Wild-eddying swirl,
Or thro' the mining outlet bocked,[4]   [4]vomited
      Down headlong hurl.

List'ning the doors an' winnocks rattle,
I thought me on the ourie[5] cattle,   [5]bristling with cold
Or silly sheep, wha bide this brattle[6]   [6]noisy onset
      O' winter war,
And thro' the drift, deep-lairing sprattle,[7]   [7]scramble
      Beneath a scar.[8]   [8]cliff

Ilk happing bird, wee, helpless thing!
That, in the merry months o' spring,
Delighted me to hear thee sing,
      What comes o' thee?
Whare wilt thou cow'r thy chittering wing,
      An' close thy e'e?

Ev'n you on murd'ring errands toil'd,
Lone from your savage homes exil'd,
The blood-stain'd roost, and sheep-cote spoil'd
      My heart forgets,
While pityless the tempest wild
      Sore on you beats.

      Robert Burns

To a Mouse

On turning her up in her nest with the plough,
November 1785

Wee, sleekit, cowrin, tim'rous beastie,
O, what a panic's in thy breastie!
Thou need na start awa sae hasty,
        Wi' bickering brattle![1]
I wad be laith[2] to rin an' chase thee,
        Wi' murd'ring pattle![3]

[1]hurrying scamper   *[2]loth*   *[3]plough-staff*

I'm truly sorry man's dominion
Has broken Nature's social union,
An' justifies that ill opinion
        Which makes thee startle
At me, thy poor, earth-born companion,
        An' fellow-mortal!

I doubt na, whyles, but thou may thieve;
What then? poor beastie, thou maun live!
A daimen-icker[4] in a thrave[5]
        'S a sma' request:
I'll get a blessin wi' the lave,[6]
        And never miss't!

[4]odd ear of corn   *[5]twenty-four sheaves*   *[6]remainder*

Thy wee bit housie, too, in ruin!
Its silly wa's the win's are strewin!
An' naething, now, to big[7] a new ane,
        O' foggage[8] green!
An' bleak December's winds ensuin,
        Baith snell[9] and keen!

[7]build   *[8]coarse grass*   *[9]bitter*

Thou saw the fields laid bare an' waste,
An' weary Winter comin' fast,
An' cozie here, beneath the blast
        Thou thought to dwell,
Till crash! the cruel coulter past
        Out thro' thy cell.

That wee bit heap o' leaves an' stibble
Has cost thee mony a weary nibble!
Now thou's turn'd out, for a' thy trouble,
    But[10] house or hald,   [10]without
To thole the Winter's sleety dribble,
    An' cranreuch[11] cauld!   [11]hoar-frost

But, Mousie, thou art no thy lane,
In proving foresight may be vain:
The best-laid schemes o' Mice an' Men,
    Gang aft agley,[12]   [12]askew
An' lea'e us nought but grief and pain
    For promis'd joy!

Still thou art blest, compar'd wi' me!
The present only toucheth thee:
But, Och! I backward cast my e'e
    On prospects drear!
An' forward, tho' I canna see,
    I guess an' fear!

      Robert Burns

Poor Mailie's Elegy

Lament in rhyme, lament in prose,
Wi' saut tears tricklin' down your nose;
Our Bardie's fate is at a close,
    Past a' remead;
The last sad cape-stane of his woes;
    Poor Mailie's dead!

It's no' the loss o' warl's gear
That could sae bitter draw the tear,
Or mak' our Bardie, dowie, wear
    The mourning weed:
He's lost a friend and neebor dear
    In Mailie dead.

Thro' a' the town she trotted by him;
A lang half-mile she could descry him;
Wi' kindly bleat, when she did spy him,
　　She ran wi' speed:
A friend mair faithfu' ne'er cam' nigh him
　　Than Mailie dead.

I wat she was a sheep o' sense,
An' could behave hersel' wi' mense;[1]
I'll say't, she never brak' a fence
　　Thro' thievish greed.
Our bardie, lanely, keeps the spence[2]
　　Sin' Mailie's dead.

[1] discretion

[2] parlour

Or, if he wanders up the howe,
Her living image in her yowe,
Comes bleating to him, owre the knowe,
　　For bits o' bread,
An' down the briny pearls rowe
　　For Mailie's dead.

She was nae get[3] o' moorland tips,[4]
Wi' tauted ket,[5] an' hairy hips;
For her forbears were brought in ships
　　Frae' yont the Tweed:
A bonnier fleesh ne'er cross'd the clips[6]
　　Than Mailie's dead.

[3] offspring
[4] rams
[5] matted fleece

[6] shears

Wae worth the man wha first did shape
That vile wanchancie[7] thing—a raep!
It maks guid fellows girn an' gape,
　　Wi' chokin' dread;
An' Robin's bonnet wave wi' crape
　　For Mailie dead.

[7] unlucky

O a' ye bards on bonie Doon!
An' wha on Ayr your chanters tune!
Come, join the melancholious croon
　　O' Robin's reed!
His heart will never get aboon!
　　His Mailie's dead!

Robert Burns

'Glen' a Sheep-Dog

I ken there isna a p'int in yer heid,
   I ken that ye're auld an' ill,
An' the dogs ye focht in yer day are deid,
   An' I doot that ye've focht yer fill;
Ye're the dourest deevil in Lothian land,
But, man, the he'rt o' ye's simply grand;
Ye're done an' doited,[1] but gie's yer hand
   An' we'll thole[2] ye a whilie still.

[1] daft or in dotage
[2] endure

A daft-like character aye ye've been
   Sin the day I brocht ye hame,
When I bocht ye doon on the Caddens green
   An' gied ye a guid Scots name;
Ye've spiled the sheep and ye've chased the stirk,
An' rabbits was mair tae yer mind nor work,
An' ye've left i' the morn an' stopped till mirk,
   But I've keepit ye a' the same.

Mebbe ye're failin' an' mebbe I'm weak,
   An' there's younger dogs tae see,
But I doot that a new freen's ill tae seek,
   An' I'm thinkin' I'll let them be;
Ye've whiles been richt whaur I've thocht wrang,
Ye've liked me weel an' ye've liked me lang,
An' when there's ane o' us got tae gang—
   May the guid Lord mak' it me.

Hilton Brown

The Sailor's Wife

And are ye sure the news is true?
  And are ye sure he's weel?
Is this a time to think o' wark?
  Ye jauds, fling bye your wheel!
Is this the time to spin a thread,
  When Colin's at the door?
Rax¹ down my cloak—I'll to the quay,
  And see him come ashore.
    For there's nae luck aboot the house,
      There's nae luck ava;
    There's little pleasure in the house
      When our gudeman's awa'.

And gie to me my bigonet,²
  My bishop's satin gown;
For I maun tell the bailie's wife
  That Colin's in the town.
My Turkey slippers maun gae on,
  My hose o' pearlin blue—
It's a' to pleasure our gudeman,
  For he's baith leal and true.

Rise up and mak' a clean fireside,
  Put on the muckle pot;
Gie little Kate her button gown,
  And Jock his Sunday coat;
And mak' their shoon as black as slaes,
  Their stockin's white as snaw,—
It's a' to please my ain gudeman—
  He likes to see them braw.

There's twa fat hens upon the bauk,³
  Hae fed this month and mair;
Mak' haste and thraw⁴ their necks about,
  That Colin weel may fare;
And spread the table neat and clean—
  Gar ilka thing look braw;
For wha can tell how Colin fared
  When he was far awa'?

¹reach

²linen cap

³cross-beam

⁴wring

Sae true his heart, sae smooth his speech,
    His breath like caller air;
His very foot has music in't
    As he comes up the stair.
And will I see his face again?
    And will I hear him speak?
I'm downright dizzy wi' the thought, —
    In troth I'm like to greet!

If Colin's weel, and weel content,
    I hae nae mair to crave;
And gin I live to keep him sae.
    I'm blest aboon the lave.
And will I see his face again.
    And will I hear him speak? —
I'm downright dizzy wi' the thought, —
    In troth I'm like to greet!
      For there's nae luck aboot the house,
        There's nae luck ava;
      There's little pleasure in the house
        When our gudeman's awa'.

                  William Julius Mickle

Tam Glen

My heart is a-breaking, dear Tittie,[1]
    Some counsel unto me come len';
To anger them a' is a pity,
    But what will I do wi' Tam Glen? —

I'm thinking, wi' sic a braw fallow,
    In poortith[2] I might mak a fen'[3]
What care I in riches to wallow,
    If I mauna marry Tam Glen? —

There's Lowrie the laird o' Drumeller,
    'Gude day to you, brute' he comes ben:
He brags and he blaws o' his siller,
    But when will he dance like Tam Glen. —

[1] sister

[2] poverty
[3] shift

My Minnie[4] does constantly deave[5] me,
 And bids me beware o' young men;
They flatter, she says, to deceive me,
 But wha can think sae o' Tam Glen. —

My Daddie says, gin I'll forsake him,
 He'll gie me gude hunder marks ten:
But, if it's ordain'd I maun take him,
 O wha will I get but Tam Glen?

Yestreen at the Valentine's dealing,
 My heart to my mou' gied a sten;[6]
For thrice I drew ane without failing,
 And thrice it was written — Tam Glen. —

The last Halloween I was waukin[7]
 My droukit[8] sark-sleeve, as ye ken;
His likeness cam up the house staukin
 And the very grey breeks o' Tam Glen!

Come counsel, dear Tittie, don't tarry;
 I'll gie you my bonie black hen,
Gif ye will advise me to marry
 The lad I lo'e dearly, Tam Glen. —

Robert Burns

The Bonnie Earl of Murray

Ye Highlands, and ye Lawlands,
 O where have you been?
They have slain the Earl of Murray,
 And layd him on the green.

'Now wae be to thee, Huntly!
 And wherefore did you sae?
I bade you bring him wi' you,
 But forbade you him to slay.'

6leap

7drying
8dripping

He was a braw gallant,
   And he rid at the ring;
And the bonny Earl of Murray,
   O he might have been a king!

He was a braw gallant,
   And he play'd at the ba;
And the bonny Earl of Murray
   Was the flower amang them a'.

He was a braw gallant,[1]
   And he play'd at the glove;
And the bonny Earl of Murray,
   O he was the Queen's true-love!

     [1] handsome young man

O lang will his Lady
   Look o'er the Castle Doune,
Ere she see the Earl of Murray
   Come sounding thro' the toun!

            Anon

Sir Patrick Spens

The King sits in Dumfermline town,
   Drinking the blude-red wine;
'O whare will I get a skeely[1] skipper,
   To sail this new ship of mine?'

     [1] skilful

O up and spake an eldern knight,
   Sat at the king's right knee:
'Sir Patrick Spens is the best sailor,
   That ever sailed the sea.'

Our king has written a braid[2] letter,
   And seal'd it with his hand,
And sent it to Sir Patrick Spens,
   'Was walking on the strand.

     [2] large and folded

'To Noroway, to Noroway,
   To Noroway o'er the faem;
The King's daughter of Noroway,
   'Tis thou maun bring her hame.'

The first word that Sir Patrick read,
   Sae loud loud laughèd he;
The neist word that Sir Patrick read,
   The tear blinded his ee.

'O wha is this has done this deed,
   And tauld the King o' me.
To send us out, at this time of the year,
   To sail upon the sea?

'Be it wind, be it weet, be it hail, be it sleet,
   Our ship must sail the faem;
The King's daughter of Noroway,
   'Tis we must fetch her hame.'

They hoysed their sales on Monanday morn
   Wi' a' the speed they may;
They hae landed in Noroway
   Upon a Wodensday.

They hadna been a week, a week,
   In Noroway, but twae,
When that the lords o' Noroway
   Began aloud to say:

'Ye Scottish men spend a' our King's goud,
   And a' our Queenis fee.'
'Ye lie, ye lie, ye liars loud!
   Fu' loud I hear ye lie;

'For I brought as much white monie,
   As gane[3] my men and me,
And I brought a half-fou[4] of gude red goud,
   Out o'er the sea wi' me.

[3]suffice
[4]eighth
part of a
peck

38

'Make read, make ready—my merry men a'!
    Our gude ship sails the morn:'[5]   [5]to-morrow
'Now, ever alake,[6] my master dear,   [6]alack, alas
    I fear a deadly storm!

'I saw the new moon, late yestreen,
    Wi' the auld moon in her arm;
And if we gang to sea, master,
    I fear we'll come to harm.'

They hadna sail'd a league, a league,
    A league but barely three,
When the lift[7] grew dark, and the wind blew loud,   [7]sky
    And gurly[8] grew the sea.   [8]growling
                                                       stormy

The ankers brak, and the topmasts lap,[9]   [9]sprang
    It was sic a deadly storm;
And the waves cam o'er the broken ship
    Till a' her sides were torn.

'O where will I get a gude sailor
    To take my helm in hand,
Till I get up to the tall topmast,
    To see if I can spy land?'

'O here am I, a sailor gude,
    To take the helm in hand,
Till you go up to the tall topmast;
    But I fear you'll ne'er spy land.'

He hadna gane a step, a step,
    A step but barely ane,
When a bout[10] flew out of our goodly ship,   [10]bolt
    And the salt sea it came in.

'Gae, fetch a web o' the silken claith,
    Another o' the twine,[11]   [11]rope
And wap[12] them into our ship's side,   [12]wrap
    And let nae the sea come in.'   throw

They fetch'd a web o' the silken claith,
    Another o' the twine,
And they wapp'd them round that gude ship's side,
    But still the sea cam in.

O laith, laith,¹³ were our gude Scots lords
    To weet their cork-heel'd shoon!
But lang or a' the play was play'd
    They wat their hats aboon.

And mony was the feather bed,
That flatter'd¹⁴ on the faem;
And mony was the gude lord's son,
    That never mair cam hame.

The ladyes wrang their fingers white,
    The maidens tore their hair,
A' for the sake of their true loves,
    For them they'll see nae mair.

O lang, lang, may the ladyes sit,
    Wi' their fans into their hand,
Before they see Sir Patrick Spens
    Come sailing to the strand!

And lang, lang, may the maidens sit,
Wi' their goud kaims¹⁵ in their hair,
A' waiting for their ain dear loves!
    For them they'll see nae mair.

Half ower, half ower, to Aberdour,
    'Tis fifty fathoms deep;
And there lies gude Sir Patrick Spens,
    Wi' the Scots lords at his feet.

                                            Anon

Thomas the Rhymer

True Thomas lay on Huntlie bank;
    A ferlie[1] he spied wi' his e'e;
And there he saw a ladye bright
    Come riding down by the Eildon Tree.

      [1] marvel

Her skirt was o' the grass-green silk,
    Her mantle o' the velvet fyne;
At ilka tett[2] o' her horse's mane
    Hung fifty siller bells and nine.

      [2] tuft

True Thomas he pu'd aff his cap,
    And louted low down on his knee:
'Hail to thee, Mary, Queen of Heaven!
    For thy peer on earth could never be.'

'O no, O no, Thomas,' she said,
    'That name does not belang to me;
I'm but the Queen o' fair Elfland,
    That am hither come to visit thee.'

'Harp and carp,[3] Thomas,' she said;
    'Harp and carp along wi' me;
And if ye dare to kiss my lips,
    Sure of your bodie I will be.'

      [3] play and recite

'Betide me weal, betide me woe,
    That weird[4] shall never daunten me.'
Syne he has kiss'd her rosy lips,
    All underneath the Eildon Tree.

      [4] doom

'Now ye maun go wi' me,' she said,
    'True Thomas, ye maun go wi' me;
And ye maun serve me seven years,
    Thro' weal or woe as may chance to be.'

She's mounted on her milk-white steed,
    She's ta'en true Thomas up behind;
And aye, whene'er her bridle rang,
    The steed gaed swifter than the wind.

O they rade on, and farther on,
  The steed gaed swifter than the wind;
Until they reach'd a desert wide,
  And living land was left behind.

'Light down, light down now, true Thomas,
  And lean your head upon my knee;
Abide ye there a little space,
  And I will show you ferlies three.

'O see ye not yon narrow road,
  So thick beset wi' thorns and briers?
That is the Path of Righteousness,
  Though after it but few enquires.

'And see ye not yon braid, braid road,
  That lies across the lily leven?⁵
That is the Path of Wickedness,
  Though some call it the Road to Heaven.

⁵lawn

'And see ye not yon bonny road
  That winds about the fernie brae?
That is the Road to fair Elfland,
  Where thou and I this night maun gae.

'But, Thomas, ye sall haud your tongue,
  Whatever ye may hear or see;
For speak ye word in Elfyn-land,
  Ye'll ne'er win back to your ain countrie.'

O they rade on, and farther on,
  And they waded rivers abune the knee;
And they saw neither sun nor moon,
  But they heard the roaring of the sea.

It was mirk, mirk night, there was nae starlight,
  They waded thro' red blude to the knee;
For a' the blude that's shed on the earth
  Rins through the springs o' that countrie.

Syne they came to a garden green,
    And she pu'd an apple frae a tree:
'Take this for thy wages, true Thomas;
    It will give thee the tongue that can never lee.'

'My tongue is my ain,' true Thomas he said;
    'A gudely gift ye wad gie to me!
I neither dought[6] to buy or sell   [6]could
    At fair or tryst where I might be.

'I dought neither speak to prince or peer,
    Nor ask of grace from fair ladye!' —
'Now haud thy peace, Thomas,' she said,
    'For as I say, so must it be.'

He has gotten a coat of the even[7] cloth,   [7]smooth
    And a pair o' shoon of the velvet green;
And till seven years were gane and past,
    True Thomas on earth was never seen.

                            Anon

Wee Teeny

The last passenger steamer to sail that day from Ardrishaig was a trip from Rothesay. It was Glasgow Fair Saturday, and Ardrishaig Quay was black with people. The *Vital Spark*, in ballast, Clydeward bound, lay inside the passenger steamer, ready to start when the latter had got under weigh, and Para Handy and his mate meanwhile sat on the fo'c'sle-head of 'the smertest boat in the tred'.

Among the crowd who had got on board was a woman with eleven children. She was standing on the paddle-box counting them to make sure—five attached to the basket that had contained their food for the day, other four clinging to her gown, and one in her arms. 'Yin, twa, three, fower, and fower's eight, and twa's ten, and then there's Wee Teeny wi' her faither doon the caibin.' She was quite serene. If she could have seen that the father had no Wee Teeny with him, she would have been distracted. As it was, however, the steamer was miles on her way when a frantic woman with ten crying children all in a row behind her made a vain appeal to the Captain to go back to Ardrishaig for her lost child.

The child was discovered on the quay by the local police ten minutes after the excursion steamer had started, and just when Para Handy was about to cast off the pawls. She was somewhere about three years old, and the only fact that could be extracted from her was that her name was Teeny. There had probably not been a more contented and self-possessed person on Ardrishaig Quay that day: she sucked her thumb with an air of positive relish, smiled on the slightest provocation, and showed the utmost willingness to go anywhere with anybody.

'The poor wee cratur!' said Para Handy sympathetically. 'She minds me fearfully of my brother Cherlie's twuns. I wudna wonder but she's a twuns too; that would be the way the mistake would be made in leavin' her. I'm no' goin' to ask you, Dougie, to do anything you wudna like, but what would you be sayin' to us taking the wean wi' us and puttin' her ashore at Rothesay? Mind you, chust if you like yoursel'.'

'It's your own vessel, you're the skipper of her, and I'm sure and I have no objections, at aal at aal,' said Dougie quite heartily, and it was speedily arranged with the police that a telegram should be sent to wait the captain of the excursion steamer at Rothesay, telling him the lost child was following in the steam-lighter *Vital Spark*.

Macphail the engineer, and The Tar, kept the child in amusement with pocket-knives, oil-cans, cotton-waste, and other maritime toys, while the Captain and Dougie went hurriedly up the village for stores for the unexpected passenger.

'You'll not need that mich,' was Dougie's opinion; 'she'll fall asleep as soon as it's dark, and no' wake till we put her ashore at Rothesay.'

'Ah, but you canna be sure o' them at that age,' said the Captain. 'My brother Cherlie wass merrit on a low-country woman, and the twuns used to sit up at night and greet in the two languages, Gaelic and Gleska, till he had to put plugs in them.'

'God bless me! plugs?' said Dougie astonished.

'Ay, chust plugs,' said the Captain emphatically. 'You'll see them often. They're made of kahouchy,[1] with a bone ring on them for screwing them on and off. It's the only thing for stopping them greetin'.'

The adventures of Wee Teeny from this stage may be better told as Para Handy told it to me some time afterwards.

'To let you ken,' he said, 'I wass feared the wean would sterve. Nothing in the ship but sea biscuits and salt beef. I went into wan shop and got a quart of milk on draught, half a pound of boiled ham the same as they have at funerals, and a tin tinny For a Good Girl. Dougie wasna slack either; he went into another shop and got thruppence worth of sweeties and a jumpin'-jeck. It wass as nice a thing ass ever you saw to see the wee cratur sittin' on the hatches eatin' away and drinkin' wi' the wan hand, and laughing like anything at the jumpin'-jeck wi' the other. I never saw the ship cheerier; it wass chust sublime. If Dougie was here himsel' he would tell you. Everything

[1]caoutchouc, india-rubber

45

wass going first-rate, and I wass doon below washing my face and puttin' on my other jecket and my watch-chain oot o' respect for the passenger, when Dougie came doon in a hurry wi' a long face on him, and says—

'"She's wantin' ta-ta."

'"Mercy on us, she canna be more ta-ta than she iss unless we throw her over the side," I says to Dougie. But I went up on dake and told her she would be ta-ta in no time becaase the ship was loggin' six knots and the wind wi' us.

'"Ta-ta," says she, tuggin' my whiskers the same as if I wass merrit on her—ah, man! she wass a nice wee thing. And that good-natured! The best I could do wass to make The Tar show her the tattoo marks on his legs, and Dougie play the trump[2] and when she wass tired o' that I carried her up and doon the dake singin' "Auld Lang Syne" till she was doverin' over.

'"She's goin' to sleep noo," I says to Dougie, and we put her in my bunk wi' her clothes on. She wanted her clothes off, but I said, "Och! never mind puttin' them off, Teeny; it's only a habit." Dougie said, if he minded right, they always put up a kind of prayer at that age. "Give her a start," I says to Dougie, and he said the 23rd Psalm in Gaalic, but she didnt' understand wan word of it, and went to sleep wi' a poke o' sweeties in her hand.

'We were off Ardlamont, and Macphail wass keepin' the boat bangin' at it to get to Rothesay before the mother went oot of her wuts, when I heard a noise doon below where Teeny wass. I ran doon and found her sittin' up chokin' wi' a sweetie that wass a size too lerge for her. She wass black in the face.

'"Hut her on the back, Peter!" said Dougie.

'"Hut her yoursel'; I wudna hurt her for the world," I says, and Dougie said he wudna do it either, but he ran up for The Tar, that hasna mich feelin's, and The Tar saved her life. I'm tellin' you it wass a start! We couldna trust her below, herself, efter that, so we took her on dake again. In ten meenutes she fell down among Macphail's engines, and nearly spoiled them. She wasna hurt a bit, but Macphail's feelin's wass, for she wass wantin' the

[2] Jew's harp

46

engines to her bed wi' her. She thought they were a kind of toy. We aye keep that up on him yet.

'"My Chove! this wean's no' canny," said Dougie, and we took her up on dake again, and put up the sail to get as much speed oot of the vessel as we could for Rothesay. Dougie played the trump even-on to her, and The Tar walked on his hands till she was sore laughing at him. Efter a bit we took oor eyes off her for maybe two meenutes, and when we turned roond again Teeny wass fallin' doon into the fo'c'sle.

'"This iss the worst cargo ever we had," I says, takin' her up again no' a bit the worse. "If we don't watch her like a hawk aal the time she'll do something desperate before we reach Rothesay. She'll jump over the side or crawl doon the funnel, and we'll be black affronted."

'"I wudna say but you're right," said Dougie. We put her sittin' on the hatch wi' the jumpin'-jeck, and the tin tinny For a Good Girl, and my watch and chain, Dougie's trump, the photygraph of The Tar's lass, and Macphail's new carpet sluppers to play wi', and the three of us sat roond her watchin' she didna swallow the watch and chain.

'When I handed her over to her mother and father on Rothesay Quay, I says to them, "I'm gled I'm no' a mother; I would a hunder times sooner be a sailor."

'But it's a nice thing a wean, too; for a week efter that we missed her awful,' concluded the Captain pensively.

Neil Munro

Helen of Kirkconnell

I wish I were where Helen lies,
Night and day on me she cries;
O that I were where Helen lies,
    On fair Kirkconnell lea!

Curst be the heart that thought the thought,
And curst the hand that fired the shot,
When in my arms burd Helen dropt,
    And died to succour me!

47

O think na ye my heart was sair,
When my Love dropp'd and spak nae mair!
There did she swoon wi' meikle care,
    On fair Kirkconnell lea.

As I went down the water side,
None but my foe to be my guide,
None but my foe to be my guide,
    On fair Kirkconnell lea;

I lighted down my sword to draw,
I hackèd him in pieces sma',
I hackèd him in pieces sma',
    For her sake that died for me.

O Helen fair, beyond compare!
I'll mak a garland o' thy hair,
Shall bind my heart for evermair,
    Until the day I dee!

O that I were where Helen lies!
Night and day on me she cries;
Out of my bed she bids me rise,
    Says, 'Haste, and come to me!'

O Helen fair! O Helen chaste!
If I were with thee, I'd be blest,
Where thou lies low an' taks thy rest,
    On fair Kirkconnell lea.

I wish my grave were growing green,
A winding-sheet drawn owre my een,
And I in Helen's arms lying,
    On fair Kirkconnell lea.

I wish I were where Helen lies!
Night and day on me she cries;
And I am weary of the skies,
    For her sake that died for me.

Anon

The Twa Corbies[1]

ravens

As I was walking all alane,
I heard twa corbies making a mane:
The tane unto the tither did say,
'Whar sall we gang and dine the day?'

'—In behint yon auld fail[2] dyke   [2]turf
I wot there lies a new-slain knight;
And naebody kens that he lies there
But his hawk, his hound, and his lady fair.

'His hound is to the hunting gane,
His hawk to fetch the wild-fowl hame,
His lady's ta'en anither mate,
So we may mak' our dinner sweet.

'Ye'll sit on his white hause-bane,[3]   [3]neck
And I'll pike out his bonny blue e'en:
Wi' ac lock o' his gowden hair
We'll theek[4] our nest when it grows bare.   [4]thatch

'Mony a one for him maks mane,
But nane sall ken whar he is gane:
O'er his white banes, when they are bare,
The wind sall blaw for evermair.'

Anon

The Braw Wooer

Last May a braw wooer cam down the lang glen,
And sair wi' his love he did deave[1] me;   [1]deafen
I said, there was naething I hated like men,
The deuce gae wi'm, to believe me, believe me,
The deuce gae wi'm to believe me.

He spak o' the darts in my bonie black een,
And vow'd for my love he was dying,
I said he might die when he liked for Jean—
The Lord forgie me for lying, for lying,
The Lord forgie me for lying!

49

²farm   A weel-stocked mailen,² himsel for the laird,
And marriage aff-hand, were his proffers;
I never loot on that I kend it, or car'd,
But thought I might hae waur offers, waur offers,
But thought I might hae waur offers.

But what wad ye think? in a fortnight or less,
The deil tak his taste to gae near her!
He up the lang loan to my black cousin, Bess,
³jade   Guess ye how, the jad!³ I could bear her, could
     bear her,
Guess ye how, the jad! I could bear her.

But a' the niest week, as I petted wi' care,
⁴cattle fair   I gaed to the tryst⁴ o' Dalgarnock;
And wha but my fine fickle wooer was there,
I glowr'd as I'd seen a warlock, a warlock,
I glowr'd as I'd seen a warlock.

But owre my left shouther I gae him a blink,
Lest neebours might say I was saucy;
My wooer he caper'd as he'd been in drink,
And vow'd I was his dear lassie, dear lassie,
And vow'd I was his dear lassie.

⁵asked   I spier'd⁵ for my cousin fu' couthy and sweet,
Gin she had recovered her hearin,
⁶shapeless   And how her new shoon fit her auld schachl't⁶ feet,
But heavens! how he fell a swearing, a swearing,
But heavens! how he fell a swearing.

He begged for Gudesake, I wad be his wife,
Or else I wad kill him wi' sorrow;
So e'en to preserve the poor body in life,
I think I maun wed him tomorrow, tomorrow,
I think I maun wed him tomorrow. —

Robert Burns

The Cobbler

The auld fowk garr'd me cobble
But ma cobblin' days are duin
Syne merrit intae siller noo
I'm by wi' buits an' shuin.
The lave[1] can hae the blessin's
O' affection an' romance,
I was still amang their bauchles[2]
Had I skippit sic a chance.

[1]remainder

[2]down-at-heel shoes

The dominie had notions
Tho' the twa-some har'ly met,
While Gossip blam't the meenister
For hingin' roun' the yett.[3]
The lawyer kenn'd 'er tocher,[4]
'Twas his preevilege tae ken,
But wi' nocht save needfu' business
Was that worthy askit ben.

[3]gate
[4]what she was worth

The laird gat interestit
Suin's he saw 'er in the pew
An' cam' tae ilka service syne
Afore attendin' few.
The preacher thocht 'im pious
'Cause he did-na un'erstaun,
But the countryside gaed speechless
Gin she taen the cobbler's haun.

                    T. T. Kilbucho

The Tale of Tod Lapraik

My faither, Tam Dale, peace to his banes, was a wild, sploring lad in his young days, wi' little wisdom and little grace. He was fond of a lass and fond of a glass, and fond of a ran-dan; but I could never hear tell that he was muckle use for honest employment. Frae ae thing to anither, he listed at last for a sodger and was in the garrison of his fort, which was the first way that ony of the Dales cam to set foot upon the Bass. Sorrow upon that service! The governor brewed his ain ale; it seems it was the warst conceivable. The rock was proveesioned frae the shores with vivers,[1] the thing was ill-guided, and there were whiles when they but[2] to fish and shoot solans for their diet. To crown a', thir was the Days of the Persecution. The perishin' cauld chalmers were all occupeed wi' sants and martyrs, the saut of the yearth, of which it wasnae worthy. And though Tam Dale carried a firelock there, a single sodger, and liked a lass and a glass, as I was sayin', the mind of the man was mair just than set with his position. He had glints of the glory of the kirk; there were whiles when his dander rase to see the Lord's sants misguided, and shame covered him that he should be haulding a can'le (or carrying a firelock) in so black a business. There were nights of it when he was here on sentry, the place a' wheesht, the frosts o' winter maybe riving in the wa's, and he would hear ane o' the prisoners strike up a psalm, and the rest join in, and the blessed sounds rising from the different chalmers—or dungeons, I would raither say—so that this auld craig in the sea was like a pairt of Heev'n. Black shame was on his saul; his sins hove up before him muckle as the Bass, and above a', that chief sin, that he should have a hand in hagging and hashing at Christ's Kirk. But the truth is that he resisted the spirit. Day cam, there were the rousing companions, and his guid resolves depairtit.

In thir days, dwalled upon the Bass a man of God, Peden the Prophet was his name. Ye'll have heard tell of Prophet Peden. There was never the wale of him sinsyne, and it's a

[1]victuals   [2]behoved

52

question wi' mony if there ever was his like afore. He was wild's a peat-hag, fearsome to look at, fearsome to hear, his face like the day of judgment. The voice of him was like a solan's and dinnle'd in folks' lugs, and the words of him like coals of fire.

Now there was a lass on the rock, and I think she had little to do, for it was nae place far dacent weemen; but it seems she was bonny, and her and Tam Dale were very well agreed. It befell that Peden was in the gairden his lane at the praying when Tam and the lass cam by; and what should the lassie do but mock with laughter at the sant's devotions? He rose and lookit at the twa o' them, and Tam's knees knoitered³ thegether at the look of him. But whan he spak, it was mair in sorrow than in anger. 'Poor thing, poor thing!' says he, and it was the lass he lookit at, 'I hear you skirl and laugh,' he sayd, 'but the Lord has a deid shot prepared for you, and at that surprising judgment ye shall skirl but the ae time!' Shortly thereafter she was daundering on the craigs wi' twa-three sodgers, and it was a blawy day. There cam a gowst of wind, claught her by the coats, and awa' wi' her bag and baggage. And it was remarked by the sodgers that she gied but the ae skirl.

Nae doubt this judgment had some weicht upon Tam Dale; but it passed again and him none the better. Ae day he was flyting wi' anither sodger-lad. 'Deil hae me!' quo' Tam, for he was a profane swearer. And there was Peden glowering at him, gash an' waefu'; Peden wi' his lang chafts an' luntin'⁴ een, the maud⁵ happed about his kist, and the hand of him held out wi' the black nails upon the finger-nebs—for he had nae care of the body. 'Fy, fy, poor man!' cries he, 'the poor fool man! *Deil hae me*, quo' he; an' I see the deil at his oxter.' The conviction of guilt and grace cam in on Tam like the deep sea; he flang doun the pike that was in his hands—'I will nae mair lift arms against the cause o' Christ!' says he, and was as gude's word. There was a sair fyke⁶ in the beginning, but the governor, seeing him resolved, gied him his dischairge, and he went and dwallt and married in North Berwick,

³knocked   ⁴glowing
⁵plaid   ⁶fuss

and had aye a gude name with honest folk frae that day on.

It was in the year seeventeen hunner and sax that the Bass cam in the hands o' the Da'rymples, and there was twa men soucht the chairge of it. Baith were weel qualified, for they had baith been sodgers in the garrison, and kent the gate to handle solans, and the seasons and values of them. Forby that they were baith—or they baith seemed —earnest professors and men of comely conversation. The first of them was just Tam Dale, my faither. The second was ane Lapraik, whom the fold ca'd Tod[7] Lapraik maistly, but whether for his name or his nature I could never hear tell. Weel, Tam gaed to see Lapraik upon this business, and took me, that was a toddlin' laddie, by the hand. Tod had his dwallin' in the lang loan benorth the kirkyaird. It's a dark uncanny loan, forby that the kirk has aye had an ill name since the days o' James the Saxt and the deevil's cantrips played therein when the Queen was on the seas; and as for Tod's house, it was in the mirkest end, and was little liked by some that kenned the best. The door was on the sneck[8] that day, and me and my faither gaed straucht in. Tod was a wabster to his trade; his loom stood in the but. There he sat, a muckle fat, white hash of a man like creish,[9] wi' a kind of a holy smile that gart me scunner. The hand of him aye cawed the shuttle, but his een was steeked. We cried to him by his name, we skirled in the deid lug of him, we shook him by the shou'ther. Nae mainner o' service! There he sat on his dowp, an' cawed the shuttle and smiled like creish.

'God be guid to us,' says Tam Dale, 'this is no canny.'

He had jimp said the word, when Tod Lapraik cam to himsel'.

'Is this you, Tam?' says he. 'Haith, man! I'm blythe to see ye. I whiles fa' into a bit dwam[10] like this,' he says; 'it's frae the stamach.'

Weel, they began to crack about the Bass, and which of them twa was to get the warding o't, and little by little cam to very ill words, and twined in anger. I mind weel

[7]Fox   [8]latch
[9]grease, tallow   [10]trance

54

that as my faither and me gaed hame again, he cam ower and ower the same expression, how little he likit Tod Lapraik and his dwams.

'Dwam!' says he. 'I think folk hae brunt for dwams like yon.'

Aweel, my faither got the Bass and Tod had to go wantin'. It was remembered sinsyne what way he had ta'en the thing. 'Tam,' says he, 'ye hae gotten the better o' me aince mair, and I hope,' says he, 'ye'll find at least a' that ye expeckit at the Bass.' Which have since been thought remarkable expressions. At last the time came for Tam Dale to take young solans. This was a business he was weel used wi', he had been a craigsman frae a laddie, and trustit nane but himsel'. So there was he hingin' by a line an' speldering[11] on the craig face, whaur it's hieest and steighest.[12] Fower tenty lads were on the tap, hauldin' the line and mindin' for his signals. But whaur Tam hung there was naething but the craig and the sea belaw, and the solan's skirlin' and flying. It was a braw spring morn, and Tam whustled as he claught[13] in the young geese. Mony's the time I've heard him tell of this experience, and aye the swat ran upon the man.

It chanced, ye see, that Tam keeked up, and he was awaur of a muckle solan, and the solan pyking at the line. He thocht this by-ordinar and outside the creature's habits. He minded that ropes was unco saft things, and the solan's neb and the Bass Rock unco hard, and that two hunner feet were raither mair than he would care to fa'.

'Shoo!' says Tam. 'Awa', bird! Shoo, awa' wi' ye!' says he.

The solan keekit doon into Tam's face, and there was something unco in the creature's ee. Just the ae keek it gied, and back to the rope. But now it wrocht and warstl't like a thing dementit. There never was the solan made that wrocht as that solan wrocht; and it seemed to understand its employ brawly, birzing[14] the saft rope between the neb of it and a crunkled jag o' stane.

There gaed a cauld stend o' fear into Tam's heart.

[11]spreadeagled   [12]steepest
[13]clutched   [14]bruising

'This thing is nae bird,' thinks he. His een turnt backward in his heid and the day gaed black aboot him. 'If I get a dwam here,' he thocht, 'it's by wi' Tam Dale.' And he signalled for the lads to pu' him up.

And it seemed the solan understood about signals. For nae sooner was the signal made than he let be the rope, spried his wings, squawked out loud, took a turn flying, and dashed straucht at Tam Dale's een. Tam had a knife, he gart the cauld steel glitter. And it seemed the solan understood about knives, for nae suner did the steel glint in the sun than he gied the ae squawk, but laigher, like a body disappointit, and flegged[15] aff about the roundness of the craig, and Tam saw him nae mair. And as sune as that thing was gane, Tam's heid drapt upon his shou'ther, and they pu'd him up like a deid corp, dadding[16] on the craig.

A dram of brandy (which he went never without) broucht him to his mind, or what was left of it. Up he sat.

'Rin, Geordie, rin to the boat, mak' sure of the boat, man—rin!' he cries, 'or yon solan 'll have it awa',' says he.

The fower lads stared at ither, an' tried to whilly-wha[17] him to be quiet. But naething would satisfy Tam Dale, till ane o' them had startit on aheid to stand sentry on the boat. The ithers askit if he was for down again.

'Na,' says he, 'and neither you nor me,' says he, 'and as sune as I can win to stand on my twa feet we'll be aff frae this craig o' Sawtan.'

Sure eneuch, nae time was lost, and that was ower muckle; for before they won to North Berwick Tam was in a crying fever. He lay a' the simmer; and wha was sae kind as come speiring for him, but Tod Lapraik! Folk thocht afterwards that ilka time Tod cam near the house the fever had worsened. I kenna for that; but what I ken the best, that was the end of it.

It was about this time o' the year; my grandfaither was out at the white fishing; and like a bairn, I but to gang wi' him. We had a grand take, I mind, and the way that the fish lay broucht us near in by the Bass, whaur we

[15]flapped   [16]knocking   [17]coax

56

foregaithered[18] wi' anither boat that belanged to a man Sandie Fletcher in Castleton. He's no lang deid neither, or ye could speir at himsel'. Weel, Sandie hailed.

'What's yon on the Bass?' says he.

'On the Bass?' says grandfaither.

'Ay,' says Sandie, 'on the green side o't.'

'Whatten kind of a thing?' says grandfaither. 'There cannae be naething on the Bass but just the sheep.'

'It looks unco like a body,' quo' Sandie, who was nearer in.

'A body!' says we, and we none of us likit that. For there was nae boat that could have brought a man, and the key o' the prison yett hung ower my faither's at hame in the press bed.

We keept the twa boats close for company, and crap in nearer hand. Grandfaither had a gless, for he had been a sailor, and the captain of a smack, and had lost her on the sands of Tay. And when we took the gless to it, sure eneuch there was a man. He was in a crunkle[19] o' green brae, a wee below the chaipel, a' by his lee lane, and lowped and flang and danced like a daft quean at a waddin'.

'It's Tod,' says grandfaither, and passed the gless to Sandie.

'Ay, it's him,' says Sandie.

'Or ane in the likeness o' him,' says grandfaither.

'Sma' is the differ,' quo' Sandie. 'De'il or warlock, I'll try the gun at him,' quo' he, and broucht up a fowling-piece that he aye carried, for Sandie was a notable famous shot in all that country.

'Haud your hand, Sandie,' says grandfaither; 'we maun see clearer first,' says he, 'or this may be a dear day's wark to the baith of us.'

'Hout!' says Sandie, 'this is the Lord's judgment surely, and be damned to it,' says he.

'Maybe ay, and maybe no,' says my grandfaither, worthy man! 'But have you a mind of the Procurator Fiscal, that I think ye'll have foregaithered wi' before,' says he.

This was ower true, and Sandie was a wee thing set ajee.

[18]met   [19]wrinkle

'Aweel, Edie,' says he, 'and what would be your way of it?'

'Ou, just this,' says grandfaither. 'Let me that has the fastest boat gang back to North Berwick, and let you bide here and keep an eye on Thon. If I cannae find Lapraik, I'll join ye and the twa of us'll have a crack wi' him. But if Lapraik's at hame, I'll rin up the flag at the harbour, and ye can try Thon Thing wi' the gun.'

Aweel, so it was agreed between them twa. I was just a bairn, an' clum in Sandie's boat, whaur I thocht I would see the best of the employ. My grandsire gied Sandie a siller tester[20] to put in his gun wi' the leid draps, bein mair deidly again bogles. And then the ae boat set aff for North Berwick, an' the tither lay whaur it was and watched the wanchancy thing on the brae-side.

A' the time we lay there it lowped and flang and capered and span like a teetotum, and whiles we could hear it skelloch[21] as it span. I hae seen lassies, the daft queans, that would lowp and dance a winter's nicht, and still be lowping and dancing when the winter's day cam in. But there would be fowk there to hauld them company, and the lads to egg them on; and this thing was its lee-lane. And there would be a fiddler diddling his elbock in the chimney-side; and this thing had nae music but the skirling of the solans. And the lassies were bits o' young things wi' the reid life dinnling and stending in their members; and this was a muckle, fat creishy man, and him fa'n in the vale o' years. Say what ye like, I maun say what I believe. It was joy was in the creature's heart, the joy o' hell, I daursay: joy whatever. Mony a time I have askit mysel' why witches and warlocks should sell their sauls (whilk are their maist dear possessions) and be auld, duddy, wrunkl't wives or auld, feckless, doddered men; and then I mind upon Tod Lapraik dancing a' the hours by his lane in the black glory of his heart. Nae doubt they burn for it muckle in hell, but they have a grand time here of it, whatever!—and the Lord forgie us!

Weel, at the hinder end, we saw the wee flag yirk up to the mast-heid upon the harbour rocks. That was a' Sandie waited for. He up wi' the gun, took a deleeberate aim, an'

[20]sixpence   [21]yell

58

pu'd the trigger. There cam' a bang and then ae waefu'
skirl frae the Bass. And there were we rubbing' our een and
looking' at ither like daft folk. For wi' the bang and the
skirl the thing had clean disappeared. The sun glintit, the
wund blew, and there was the bare yaird whaur the
Wonder had been lowping and flinging but ae second syne.

The hale way hame I roared and grat wi' the terror o'
that dispensation. The grown folk were nane sae muckle
better; there was little said in Sandie's boat but just the
name of God; and when we won in by the pier, the
harbour rocks were fair black wi' the folk waitin' us. It
seems they had fund Lapraik in ane on his dwams,
cawing the shuttle and smiling. Ae lad they sent to hoist
the flag, and the rest abode there in the wabster's house.
You may be sure they liked it little; but it was a means of
grace to severals that stood there praying in to themsel's
(for nane cared to pray out loud) and looking on thon
awesome thing as it cawed the shuttle. Syne, upon a sud-
denty, and wi' the ae dreidfu' skelloch, Tod sprang up
frae his hinderlands and fell forrit on the wab, a bluidy
corp.

When the corp was examined the leid draps hadnae
played buff upon the warlock's body; sorrow a leid drap
was to be fund! but there was grandfaither's siller tester
in the puddock's heart of him.

R. L. Stevenson

Poaching in Excelsis

'Two men were fined £120 a-piece for poaching white rhinoceros.'—
Times of Africa.

I've poached a pickle pairtricks when the leaves
were turnin' sere,
I've poached a twa-three hares an' groose, an'
mebbe whiles a deer,
But ou, it seems an unco thing, an' jist a wee
mysterious
Hoo ony mortal could contrive tae poach a
rhinocerious.

I've crackit wi' the keepers, pockets packed wi'
pheasant's eggs,
An' a ten-pun' saumon hangin' doun in baith my
trouser legs.
But eh, I doot effects wud be a wee thing dele-
terious
Gin ye shuld stow intil yer breeks a brace o'
rhinocerious.

I mind hoo me an' Wullie shot a Royal in Braemar,
An' brocht him doun tae Athol by the licht o'
mune an' star.
An' eh, sirs! but the canny beast contrived tae fash
an' weary us—
Yet staigs maun be but bairn's play beside a
rhinocerious.

I thocht I kent o' poachin' jist as muckle's ither
men,
But there is still a twa-three things I doot I dinna
ken,
An' noo I canna rest, my brain is growin' that
deleerious
Tae win awa' tae Africa an' poach a rhinocerious.

G. K. Menzies

60

The Laird o' Cockpen

The Laird o' Cockpen, he's proud an' he's great,
His mind is ta'en up wi' things o' the State:
He wanted a wife, his braw house to keep;
But favour wi' wooin' was fashious[1] to seek.   [1]troublesome

Down by the dyke-side a lady did dwell;
At his table-head he thought she'd look well—
McClish's ae daughter o' Clavers-ha' Lee,
A penniless lass wi' a lang pedigree.

His wig was weel pouther'd and as gude as new,
His waistcoat was white, his coat it was blue;
He put on a ring, a sword, and cock'd hat,
And wha could refuse the Laird wi' a' that?

He took the grey mare, and rade cannily,
An' rapp'd at the yett o' Clavers-ha' Lee;
'Gae tell Mistress Jean to come speedily ben,
She's wantit to speak to the Laird o' Cockpen.'

Mistress Jean she was makin' the elder-flower wine;
'And what brings the Laird at sic a like time?'
She put aff her apron and on her silk goun,
Her mutch wi' red ribbons, and gaed awa doun.

An' when she cam' ben he bowed fu' low,
An' what was his errand he soon let her know;
Amazed was the Laird when the lady said 'Na',
And wi' a laigh curtsie she turned awa.

Dumbfounder'd was he, but nae sigh did he gie,
He mounted his mare—he rade cannilie;
An' aften he thought, as he gaed thro' the glen,
'She's daft to refuse the Laird o' Cockpen!'

Lady Nairne

Duncan Gray

Duncan Gray cam' here to woo,
  Ha, ha, the wooing o't,
On blythe Yule night when we were fu,
  Ha, ha, the wooing o't.
Maggie coost her head fu' high,
Look'd asklent and unco skeigh,[1]
Gart poor Duncan stand abeigh,[2]
  Ha, ha, the wooing o't.

Duncan fleech'd,[3] and Duncan pray'd;
  Ha, ha, the wooing o't;
Meg was deaf as Ailsa Craig,
  Ha, ha, the wooing o't.
Duncan sigh'd baith out and in,
Grat his een baith bleer't and blin',
Spak o' lowpin o'er a linn;
  Ha, ha, the wooing o't.

Time and Chance are but a tide,
  Ha, ha, the wooing o't.
Slighted love is sair to bide,
  Ha, ha, the wooing o't.
Shall I, like a fool, quoth he,
For a haughty hizzie die?
She may gae to—France for me!
  Ha, ha, the wooing o't.

How it comes let Doctors tell,
  Ha, ha, the wooing o't.
Meg grew sick as he grew hale,
  Ha, ha, the wooing o't.
Something in her bosom wrings,
For relief a sigh she brings;
And O, her een, they spak sic things!
  Ha, ha, the wooing o't.

[1]disdainful
[2]aloof
[3]begged

Duncan was a lad o' grace,
   Ha, ha, the wooing o't.
Maggie's was a piteous case,
   Ha, ha, the wooing o't.
Duncan could na be her death,
Swelling pity smoor'd[4] his wrath;   [4]smothered
Now they're crouse and canty[5] baith,   [5]gleeful
   Ha, ha, the wooing o't.

Robert Burns

There's a Fairmer that I Ken o'

There's a fairmer that I ken o',
An' he's jist fut[1] he should be,   [1]what
For he disna gyang[2] te mart an' roup,   [2]go
Te taste the barley-bree,[3]   [3]whisky
But dells his gairden-grun',
Till the swite[4] draps fae his beard,   [4]sweat
For the dockens aye growe heichest,[5] [5]highest
In a Buchan fairmer's yaird.

The servant lads — they lo'e him well,
They a' get halesome maet,
Nae yavel broth! but pork and beef,
an' dumplings steamin' het;
An' fyles[6] a roastit turkey   [6]at times
wi' stuffin' but an' ben,
For there's naething they like better,
Than the stappin' o' a hen.

An' fin[7] the wither's weety,   [7]when
He tak's them a' in by,
Faur they a' get cups o' warm tay,
An' buttered scones forbye.
He disna hain[8] the bottle   [8]save
Fin there's hairstin' te be done,
An' he nivver keeps them workin',
By the ried licht o' the mune.

And O the chaumer's bonnie!
For there's pintit on the wa's,
Horsies, dyucks an' grumphies[9]
A' rinnin doon in raws:
There's a gweed[10] aul'-fashioned sofa,
Faur the foreman can lie doon,
Twa airm-chairs wi' cushions,
An' a humpty[11] for the loon.[12]

O this fairmer that I ken o',
Is an elder o' the kirk,
An' pits as muckle in the plate,
Wad buy a growein' stirk,
His name I canna tell ye,
He's a man I nivver met,
In a' the land o' Buchan,
For—he's nae born yet!

J. C. Milne

[9]ducks and pigs
[10]good
[11]cushion-seat
[12]young farm-worker

Tam o' Shanter. A Tale

When chapman billies leave the street,
And drouthy neebors, neebors meet,
As market-days are wearin late,
An' folk begin to tak the gate;
While we sit bousing at the nappy,[1]
An' gettin' fou and unco happy,
We think na on the lang Scots miles,
The mosses, waters, slaps,[2] and styles,
That lie between us and our hame,
Whare sits our sulky, sullen dame,
Gathering her brows like gathering storm,
Nursing her wrath to keep it warm.

    This truth fand honest Tam o' Shanter,
As he frae Ayr ae night did canter,
(Auld Ayr, wham ne'er a town surpasses,
For honest men an' bonny lasses.)

[1]ale
[2]gaps

64

O Tam! hadst thou but been sae wise,
As ta'en thy ain wife Kate's advice!
She tauld thee weel thou wast a skellum,[3]
A blethering, blustering, drunken blellum;[4]
That frae November till October,
Ae market-day thou was na sober;
That ilka melder,[5] wi' the miller,
Thou sat as lang as thou had siller;
That every naig was ca'd a shoe on,
The smith and thee gat roaring fou on;
That at the Lord's house, even on Sunday,
Thou drank wi' Kirkton Jean till Monday.
She prophesied that, late or soon,
Thou wad be found, deep drown'd in Doon;
Or catch'd wi' warlocks in the mirk,
By Alloway's auld, haunted kirk.

[3]ne'er-do-weel
[4]babbler

[5]grinding

Ah, gentle dames! it gars me greet
To think how mony counsels sweet,
How mony lengthen'd sage advices,
The husband frae the wife despises!

But to our tale: Ae market night,
Tam had got planted unco right;
Fast by an ingle, bleezing finely,
Wi' reaming swats,[6] that drank divinely;
An' at his elbow, Souter Johnny,
His ancient, trusty, drouthy crony;
Tam lo'ed him like a vera brither;
They had been fou for weeks thegither.
The night drave on wi' sangs an' clatter;
An' aye the ale was growing better:
The landlady and Tam grew gracious,
Wi' favours secret, sweet, and precious;
The Souter tauld his queerest stories;
The landlord's laugh was ready chorus:
The storm without might rair and rustle,
Tam didna mind the storm a whistle.

[6]foaming ale

Care, mad to see a man sae happy,
E'en drown'd himsel amang the nappy:
As bees flee hame wi' lades o' treasure,
The minutes wing'd their way wi' pleasure:
Kings may be blest, but Tam was glorious,
O'er a' the ills o' life victorious!

But pleasures are like poppies spread,
You seize the flow'r, its bloom is shed;
Or like the snow falls in the river,
A moment white—then melts for ever;
Or like the borealis race,
That flit ere you can point their place;
Or like the rainbow's lovely form
Evanishing amid the storm.—
Nae man can tether time or tide;
The hour approaches Tam maun ride;
That hour, o' night's black arch the key-stane,
That dreary hour he mounts his beast in;
An' sic a night he taks the road in,
As ne'er poor sinner was abroad in.

The wind blew as 'twad blawn its last;
The rattling showers rose on the blast;
The speedy gleams the darkness swallow'd;
Loud, deep, and lang, the thunder bellow'd:
That night, a child might understand,
The Deil had business on his hand.

Weel mounted on his grey mare, Meg,
A better never lifted leg,
Tam skelpit on thro' dub an' mire,
Despising wind, and rain, and fire;
Whiles holding fast his gude blue bonnet;
Whiles crooning o'er some auld Scots sonnet;
Whiles glowring round wi' prudent cares,
Lest bogles catch him unawares:
Kirk-Alloway was drawing nigh,
Where ghaists and houlets nightly cry.—

By this time he was cross the ford,
Whare, in the snaw, the chapman smoor'd;
And past the birks and meikle stane,
Whare drunken Charlie brak's neck-bane;
And thro' the whins, and by the cairn,
Whare hunters fand the murder'd bairn;
And near the thorn, aboon the well,
Whare Mungo's mither hang'd hersel. —
Before him Doon pours a' his floods;
The doubling storm roars thro' the woods;
The lightnings flash from pole to pole;
Near and more near the thunders roll;
When, glimmering thro' the groaning trees,
Kirk-Alloway seem'd in a bleeze;
Thro' ilka bore[7] the beams were glancing;   [7]hole
An' loud resounded mirth and dancing.
Inspiring bold John Barleycorn!
What dangers thou canst mak us scorn!
Wi' tippenny, we fear nae evil;
Wi' usquabae we'll face the devil! —
The swats sae ream'd in Tammie's noddle,
Fair play, he car'd na deils a boddle.
But Maggie stood right sair astonish'd,
Till, by the heel an' hand admonish'd,
She ventured forward on the light;
An', wow! Tam saw an unco sight!
Warlocks and witches in a dance;
Nae cotillion brent new frae France,
But hornpipes, jigs, strathspeys, an' reels,
Put life an' mettle in their heels.
A winnock-bunker[8] in the east,   [8]window-
There sat auld Nick, in shape o' beast;   seat
A towzie tyke, black, grim an' large,
To gie them music was his charge:
He screw'd the pipes and gart them skirl,
Till roof and rafters a' did dirl.[9] —   [9]vibrate
Coffins stood round, like open presses,
That shaw'd the dead in their last dresses;
And by some devilish cantraip sleight
Each in its cauld hand held a light. —

By which heroic Tam was able
To note upon the haly table,
A murderer's banes in gibbet airns;
Twa span-lang, wee, unchristen'd bairns;
A thief, new-cutted frae a rape.
Wi' his last gasp his gab did gape;
Five tomahawks, wi' blude red-rusted;
Five scymitars, wi' murder crusted;
A garter, which a babe had strangled;
A knife, a father's throat had mangled,
Whom his ain son o' life bereft,
The grey hairs yet stack to the heft;
Wi' mair o' horrible an' awfu',
Which even to name wad be unlawfu'.

As Tammie glowr'd, amaz'd, and curious,
The mirth and fun grew fast and furious:
The piper loud and louder blew,
The dancers quick and quicker flew;
[10]linked arms They reel'd, they set, they cross'd, they cleekit,[10]
Till ilka carlin swat and reekit,
And coost her duddies to the wark
[11]went briskly And linket[11] at it in her sark!

Now Tam, O Tam! had thae been queans,
A' plump and strapping in their teens;
[12]greasy Their sarks, instead o' creeshie[12] flannen,
Been snaw-white seventeen hunder linnen!
Thir breeks o' mine, my only pair,
That ance were plush, o' guid blue hair,
[13]hips I wad hae gi'en them aff my hurdies,[13]
For ae blink o' the bonie burdies!

But withered beldams, auld and droll,
[14]tough Rigwoodie[14] hags, wad spean[15] a foal,
[15]wean
[16]staff with Lowping an' flinging on a crummock,[16]
crooked head I wonder didna turn thy stomach.

But Tam kenn'd what was what fu' brawlie,
There was ae winsome wench an' wawlie,[17]   [17]spirited
That night enlisted in the core,[18]   [18]corps
(Lang after ken'd on Carrick shore;
For mony a beast to dead she shot,
And perish'd mony a bonny boat,
And shook baith meikle corn and bear,
And kept the country-side in fear:)
Her cutty sark, o' Paisley harn,[19]   [19]coarse flax
That, while a lassie, she had worn,
In longitude tho' sorely scanty,
It was her best, an' she was vauntie. —
Ah! little kend thy reverend grannie,
That sark she coft for her wee Nannie,
Wi' twa pund Scots ('twas a' her riches),
Wad ever grac'd a dance of witches!

But here my Muse her wing maun cour;
Sic flights are far beyond her pow'r;
To sing how Nannie lap and flang,
(A souple jade she was, and strang),
And how Tam stood, like ane bewitch'd,
And thought his very een enrich'd;
Even Satan glowr'd, an' fidg'd fu' fain,
And hotched[20] and blew wi' might and main: [20]fidgeted
Till first ae caper, syne anither,
Tam tint his reason a' thegither,
And roars out, 'Weel done, Cutty-sark!'
And in an instant all was dark:
And scarcely had he Maggie rallied,
When out the hellish legion sallied.

As bees bizz out wi' angry fyke,[21]   [21]fuss
When plunderin' herds assail their byke;
As open pussie's mortal foes,
When, pop! she starts before their nose;
As eager runs the market-crowd,
When 'Catch the thief!' resounds aloud;
So Maggie runs, the witches follow,
Wi' mony an eldritch[22] screech an' hollow.   [22]unearthly

69

Ah, Tam! Ah, Tam! thou'll get thy fairin'![23]
In hell they'll roast thee like a herrin!
In vain thy Kate awaits thy comin!
Kate soon will be a woefu' woman!
Now, do thy speedy utmost, Meg,
And win the key-stane o' the brig;
There at them thou thy tail may toss,
A running stream they dare na cross.
But ere the key-stane she could make,
The fient a tail she had to shake!
For Nannie, far before the rest,
Hard upon noble Maggie prest,
24intent And flew at Tam wi' curious ettle,[24]
But little wist she Maggie's mettle—
Ae spring brought off her master hale,
But left behind her ain grey tail:
25clutched The carlin claught[25] her by the rump,
And left poor Maggie scarce a stump.

Now, wha this tale o' truth shall read,
Ilk man and mother's son take heed:
Whene'er to drink you are inclin'd,
Or cutty-sarks run in your mind,
Think! ye may buy the joys o'er dear—
Remember Tam o' Shanter's mare.

                                    Robert Burns

Home Thoughts from Abroad

Aifter the war, says the papers, they'll no be content at
hame,
The lads that hae feucht wi' death twae 'ear i' the mud
and the rain and the snaw;
For aifter a sodger's life the shop will be unco tame;
They'll ettle at fortune and freedom in the new lands
far awa'.

No me!
By God! No me!
Aince we hae lickit oor faes
And aince I get oot o' this hell,
For the rest o' my leevin days
I'll mak a pet o' mysel'.
I'll haste me back wi' an eident[1] fit   [1]eager
And settle again in the same auld bit.
And oh! the comfort to snowk[2] again   [2]snuff
The reek o' my mither's but-and-ben,
The wee box-bed and the ingle neuk
And the kail-pat hung frae the chimley-heuk!
I'll gang back to the shop like a laddie to play,
Tak doun the shutters at skreigh[3] o' day,   [3]break
And weigh oot floor wi' a carefu' pride,
And hear the clash[4] o' the countraside.   [4]gossip
I'll wear for ordinar' a roond hard hat,
A collar and dicky and black cravat.
If the weather's wat I'll no stir ootbye
Wi' oot an umbrella to keep me dry.
I think I'd better no tak a wife—
I've had a' the adventure I want in life.—
But at nicht, when the doors are steeked, I'll sit,
While the bleeze loups high frae the aiken ruit,
And smoke my pipe aside the crook,[5]   [5]pot-hook
And read in some douce auld-farrant[6] book;   [6]old-
Or crack wi' Davie and mix a rummer,   fashioned
While the auld wife's pow nid-nods in slum'er;
And hark to the winds gaun tearin' bye
And thank the Lord I'm sae warm and dry.

When simmer brings the lang bricht e'en,
I'll daunder doun to the bowling-green,
Or delve my yaird and my roses tend
⁷autumn   For the big floo'er-show in the next back-end.[7]
Whiles, when the sun blinks aifter rain,
I'll tak my rod and gang up the glen;
Me and Davie, we ken the püles
Whaur the troot grow great in the howes o' the hills;
And, wanderin' back when the gloamin' fa's
And the midges dance in the hazel shaws,
We'll stop at the yett ayont the hicht
And drink great wauchts o' the scented nicht,
While the hoose lamps kin'le raw by raw
And a yellow star hings ower the law.
Davie will lauch like a wean at a fair
And nip my airm to mak certain shüre
That we're back frae yon place o' dule and dreid,
To oor ain kind warld—

But Davie's deid!
Nae mair gude nor ill can betide him.
We happit him doun by Beaumont toun,
⁸mould   *And the half o' my hert's in the mools[8] aside him.*

John Buchan

Bonnie Dundee

To the Lords of Convention 'twas Claver'se who
    spoke,
'Ere the King's crown shall fall there are crowns to
    be broke;
So let each Cavalier who loves honour and me,
Come follow the bonnet of Bonnie Dundee.'
   'Come fill up my cup, come fill up my can,
    Come saddle your horses and call up your men;
    Come open the West Port, and let me gang free,
    And it's room for the bonnets of Bonnie Dundee!'

Dundee he is mounted, he rides up the street,
The bells are rung backward, the drums they are
beat;
But the Provost, douce man, said 'Just e'en let
him be,
The Gude Town is weel quit of that Deil of
Dundee.'
'Come fill up my cup,' &c.

With sour-featured Whigs the Grass Market was
cramm'd,
As if half the West had set tryst to be hang'd;
There was spite in each look, there was fear in
each e'e,
As they watched for the bonnets of Bonnie Dundee.
'Come fill up my cup,' &c.

These cowls of Kilmarnock had spits and had
spears,
And lang-hafted gullies to kill Cavaliers;
But they shrunk to close-heads, and the causeway
was free,
At the toss of the bonnet of Bonnie Dundee.
'Come fill up my cup,' &c.

He spurr'd to the foot of the proud Castle rock,
And with the gay Gordon he gallantly spoke;
'Let Mons Meg and her marrows speak twa words
or three,
For the love of the bonnet of Bonnie Dundee.'
'Come fill up my cup,' &c.

The Gordon demands of him which way he goes—
'Where'er shall direct me the shade of Montrose.
Your Grace in short space shall hear tidings of me,
Or that low lies the bonnet of Bonnie Dundee.'
'Come fill up my cup,' &c.

'There are hills beyond Pentland, lands beyond
    Forth;
If there's lords in the Lowlands, there's chiefs in
    the North;
There are wild Duniewassals,[1] three thousand
    times three,
Will cry *hoigh* for the bonnet of Bonnie Dundee.'
    'Come fill up my cup,' &c.

[1] Highland gentlemen

'There's brass on the target of barken'd[2] bull-hide;
There's steel in the scabbard that dangles beside;
The brass shall be burnish'd, the steel shall flash
    free,
At a toss of the bonnet of Bonnie Dundee.'
    'Come fill up my cup,' &c.

[2] tanned

'Away to the hills, to the caves, to the rocks—
Ere I own an usurper, I'll couch with the fox;
And tremble, false Whigs, in the midst of your glee,
You have not seen the last of my bonnet and me!'
    'Come fill up my cup,' &c.

He waved his proud hand, and the trumpets were
    blown,
The kettle-drums clash'd, and the horsemen rode
    on,
Till on Ravelston's cliffs and on Clermiston's lee
Died away the wild war-notes of Bonnie Dundee.
    'Come fill up my cup, come fill up my can,
    Come saddle the horses and call up the men,
    Come open your gates and let me gae free,
    For it's up with the bonnets of Bonnie Dundee!'

                                        Sir Walter Scott

The Image o' God

Crawlin' aboot like a snail in the mud,
Covered wi' clammy blae,[1]   [1]blue mud
ME, made after the image of God—
Jings! but it's laughable, tae.

Howkin' awa' 'neath a mountain o' stane,
Gaspin' for want o' air.
The sweat makin' streams doon my bare back-bane,
And my knees a' hauckit and sair.

Strainin' and cursin' the hale shift through,
Half-starved, half-blin, half-mad;
And the gaffer[2] he says, 'Less dirt in that coal   [2]foreman
Or ye go up the pit, my lad!'

So I gi'e my life to the Nimmo squad,
For eicht and fower a day;
ME! made after the image o' God—
Jings! but it's laughable, tae.

                                    Joe Corrie

Look Up to Pentland's Tow'ring Tap

Look up to Pentland's tow'ring tap,
    Buried beneath big wreaths o' snaw,
O'er ilka cleugh, ilk scar an' slap,
    As high as ony Roman wa'.

Driving their ba's frae whins or tee,
    There's no ae gowfer to be seen;
Nor douser fouk, wysing a-jee[1]   [1]turning
    The byas bouls on Tamson's green.   aslant

Then fling on coals, an' ripe the ribs,
    An' beek[2] the house baith butt an' ben;   [2]warm
That mutchkin-stoup it hauds but dribs,
    Then let's get in the tappit hen.

D   75

Guid claret best keeps out the cauld,
  An' drives awa the winter soon;
³shrewd   It maks a man baith gash³ an' bauld,
  An' heaves his saul ayont the moon.

Leave to the gods your ilka care;
  If that they think us worth their while,
They can a rowth o' blessings spare,
  Which will our fashious fears beguile.

For what they hae a mind to do,
  That will they do, shoul'd we gang wud;
If they command the storms to blaw,
  Then upo' sight the hailstanes thud.

                    Allan Ramsay

The Coo Park

I'm echty-five; and frae I was a bairn
I never mind the coo park 'neth the ploo;
And, when I saw the cou'ter tearing' 't thro',
Deep in my very hairt I felt the airn.
Gin the auld maister in his grave could lairn
O' this, he wad be mad. It never grew
But tails tae cattle beasts. And here it's noo—
¹dung They want a crap o' tatties oot the shairn.¹

Ay, weel-a-wat, I've lived ayont my lease:
Auld days, auld ways, auld things are at an end.
The war has finished a'; and ne'er will peace
Bring back tae me the auld warld that I kenned.
Ay, when that airman landed on the coo,
I jist said tae mysel', *We've come till't noo.*

                    Andrew Dodds

It Wasna His Wyte

It wasna his wyte[1] he was beddit sae late
  An' him wi' sae muckle to dee,
He'd the rabbits to feed an' the fulpie[2] to kame
  An' the hens to hish[3] into the ree;
The mason's mear[4] syne he set up in the closs
  An' coupit[5] the ladle fu' keen,
An' roon the ruck foun's[6] wi' the lave o' the loons
  Played 'Takie' by licht o' the meen.
Syne he rypit[7] his pooches an' coontit his bools,
  The reid-cheekit pitcher an' a',
Took the yirlin's[8] fower eggs fae his bonnet, an', fegs,
  When gorbell't[9] they're fykie to blaw;
But furth cam' his mither an' cried on him in,
  Tho' sairly he priggit[10] to wait —
'The'll be nae wird o' this in the mornin', my
    laad' —
  But it wasna his wyte he was late.

'Och, hey!' an' 'Och hum!' he was raxin' himsel'
  An' rubbin' his een when he raise,
An' faur was his bonnet an' faur was his beets
  An' fa had been touchin' his claes?
Ach! his porritch was caul', they'd forgotten the
    saut,
  There was owre muckle meal on the tap,
Was this a' the buttermilk, faur was his speen,
  An' fa had been bitin' his bap?'
His pints[11] wasna tied, an' the backs o' his lugs
  Nott[12] some sma' attention as weel—
But it wasna as gin it was Sabbath, ye ken,
  An' onything does for the squeel.
Wi' his piece in his pooch he got roadit at last,
  Wi' his beuks an' his skaalie[13] an' sklate,
Gin the wag-at-the-wa' in the kitchie was slaw—
  Weel, it wasna his wyte he was late.

[1] blame
[2] little whelp or puppy
[3] run
[4] trestle
[5] played see-saw
[6] haystack foundations
[7] ransacked
[8] yellow-hammer
[9] with young in them
[10] begged
[11] boot-laces
[12] needed
[13] slate-pencil

The fite-fuskered cat wi' her tail in the air
   Convoyed him as far as the barn,
Syne, munchin' his piece, he set aff by his leen,
   Tho' nae very willin', I'se warn'.
The cairt road was dubby, the track throu' the wid,
   Altho' maybe langer, was best,
But when loupin' the dyke a steen-chackert[14] flew oot,
   An' he huntit a fyle for her nest.
Syne he cloddit wi' yowies[15] a squirrel he saw
   Teetin' roon fae the back o' a tree,
An' jinkit the 'Gamie,' oot teeming his girns[16]—
   A ragie aul' billie was he.
A' this was a hinner; an' up the moss side
   He ran noo at siccan a rate
That he fell i' the heather an' barkit his shins,
   Sae it wasna his wyte he was late.

Astride on a win'-casten larick[17] he sat
   An' pykit for rosit to chaw,
Till a pairtick, sair frichtened, ran trailin' a wing
   Fae her cheepers to tryst him awa'.
He cried on the dryster[18] when passin' the mull,
   Got a lunt[19] o' his pipe an' a news,
An' his oxter pooch managed wi' shillans[20] to full—
   A treat to tak' hame till his doos.
Syne he waded the lade an' crap under the brig
   To hear the gigs thunner abeen,
An' a rotten plumped in an' gaed swimmin' awa'
   Afore he could gaither a steen.
He hovered to herrie a foggies bees'[21] byke
   Nae far fae the mole-catcher's gate,
An' the squeel it was in or he'd coontit his stangs—
   But it wasna his wyte he was late.

[14]stonechat

[15]fir-cones

[16]emptying his snares

[17]larch

[18]kiln-man

[19]whiff

[20]oat kernels

[21]humble-bee

78

He tried on his taes to creep ben till his seat,
  But the snuffy aul' Dominie saw,
Sneckit there in his dask like a wyver that waits
  For a flee in his wob on the wa';
He tell't o' his tum'le, but fat was the eese
  Wi' the mannie in sic an ill teen,
An' fat was a wap wi' a spainyie or tag[22]
  To hands that were hard as a steen?
Noo, gin he had grutten, it's brawly he kent
  Foo croose a' the lassies would craw,
For the mornin' afore he had scattered their lames,[23]
  An' dung doon their hoosies an' a'.
Wi' a gully to hooie[24] tho', soon he got owre
  The wye he'd been han'led by fate,
It was coorse still an' on[25] to be walloped like thon,
  When it wasna his wyte he was late.

It's thirly year, said ye, it's forty an' mair,
  Sin' last we were licket at squeel;
The Dominie's deid, an' forgotten for lang,
  An' a' oor buik learnin' as weel.
The size o' a park — wi' the gushets[26] left oot —
  We'll guess geyan near, I daur say;
Or the wecht o' a stot, but we wouldna gyang far
  Ging we tried noo the coontin' in 'Gray'.[27]
'Effectual Callin' we canna rin throu'
  Wha kent it aince clear as the text,
We can say 'Man's Chief En' an' the shorter
    'Commands',
  But fat was the 'Reasons Annexed'?
Oor heads micht be riddels for a' they haud in
  O' Catechis, coontin' or date,
Yet I'll wauger we min' on the mornin's lang syne
  When it wasna oor wyte we were late.

Charles Murray

[22]cane or strap

[23]broken earthenware

[24]barter

[25]nevertheless

[26]gussets

[27]Gray's Arithmetic

The Boy's September

Whase wheat was the ripest he brawly could tell,
  And lang ere a heuk had been laid to the crap;
He sampled the neeps, wi' the best for himsel',
  And the warst for his butty,[1] kee-vee[2] at the slap.

The black-stackit, weel teuched[3] bean was his joy,
  To pouch at the dark'nin', and scoor[4] for the yett;
It wasna the beans but the risk o' the ploy,
  And the nearer to catchin' the sweeter they e't.

He kent whaur the thistle had hoddin his cheese
  When his weel-huakit[5] gully had strippit the jags;
He speer't na what skep was expeckin' the bees
  That he eased o' the burden that wechtit their bags.

For the blaeberry law, and the rasp in the den,
  He never mislippen't[6] the time o' the year;
And ye kent when he gaed to the hazelwood glen,
  Frae his new-cuttit staff and his scarts frae the brier.

The hemlock's toom shank was a gun to his haun',
  To pock Willie's nose wi' a batt'ry of haws;
And he slang tattie plooms frae the end o' a whaun,[7]
  To fricht the bit rabbits, and bother the craws.

He learned the red rowan the dervish's skip
  On his faither's auld pipe, wi' a preen for a leg;
And he keepit the kittly wee seeds o' the hip
  To pap 'tween the shouthers o' Leezie and Meg.

And his fechts in the stooks, wi' his cheek and his brow
  War-paintit wi' bram'le! – But there let me en', –
It's aften I won'er if laddies enoo
  Ken hauf o' the fun that September was then!

Walter Wingate

[1] chum
[2] qui-vive
[3] toughened
[4] scurry
[5] well-hacked
[6] neglected
[7] thong

Tullochgorum

Come gie's a sang, the lady cry'd
And lay your disputes all aside,
What signifies't for folks to chide
For what was done before them:

Let Whig and Tory all agree,
Whig and Tory, Whig and Tory,
Whig and Tory all agree,
To drop their Whigmegmorum;[1]   [1]politics

Let Whig and Tory all agree
To spend the night wi' mirth and glee,
And cheerfu' sing alang wi' me,
The reel of Tullochgorum.

Tullochgorum's my delight,
It gars[2] us a' in ane unite,   [2]compels
And ony sumph that keeps up spite,
In conscience I abhor him.

Blithe and merry we's be a',
Blithe and merry, blithe and merry,
Blithe and merry we's be a',
To mak' a cheerfu' quorum.

Blithe and merry we's be a',
As lang as we hae breath to draw,
And dance till we be like to fa',
The reel of Tullochgorum.

There needna be sae great a phrase,[3]   [3]fracas
Wi' dringing[4] dull Italian lays,   [4]wearisome
I wadna gie our ain Strathspeys
For half a hundred score o' em;

They're douff and dowie[5] at the best,   [5]useful, sad
Douff and dowie, douff and dowie,
They're douff and dowie at the best,
Wi' a' their variorum:

They're douff and dowie at the best,
Their allegros and a' the rest,
They canna' please a Highland taste,
Compar'd wi' Tullochgorum.

Let warldly minds themselves oppress
Wi' fear of want and double cess,
And silly sauls themselves distress,
Wi' keeping up decorum:

Shall we sae sour and sulky sit,
Sour and sulky, sour and sulky,
Shall we sour and sulky sit,
Like old Philosophorum?

Shall we sae sour and sulky sit,
Wi' neither sense, nor mirth, nor wit,
And canna try to shake a fit
At the reel of Tullochgorum?

My choicest blessings still attend
Each honest open hearted friend,
And calm and quiet be his end,
Be a' that's good before him!

May peace and plenty be his lot,
Peace and plenty, peace and plenty,
Peace and plenty be his lot,
And dainties a great store o' em;

May peace and plenty be his lot,
Unstained by any vicious blot,
And may he never want a groat,
That's fond of Tullochgorum!

But for the discontented fool,
Who wants to be oppression's tool,
May envy gnaw his rotten soul,
And blackest friends devour him!

May dule[6] and sorrow be his chance,   6grief
Dule and sorrow, dule and sorrow,
Dule and sorrow be his chance,
And honest souls abhor him!

May dule and sorrow be his chance,
And a' the ills that come frae France,
Wha e'er he be that winna dance
The reel of Tullochgorum!

Rev. John Skinner

('The best Scotch song ever Scotland saw'—Robert Burns)

The Auld Doctor

O' a the jobs that sweat the sark,[1]   1shirt
Gie me a kintra[2] doctor's wark,   2country
Ye ca' awa frae dawn till dark,
Whate'er the weather be, O!

Some tinkler wife is in the strae,[3]   3straw
Your boots is owre the taps wi' clay
Through wadin' bog an' sklimmin' brae,
The besom for to see, O!

Ye ken auld Jock o' Windybarns?
The bull had near ca'ed oot his harns,[4] 4brains
His een was blinkin' fu' o' starns,[5]   5stars
An' doon they ran for me, O!

There's ae guid wife, we're weel acquaint,
Nae trouble's kent but what she's taen't,
Yet aye she finds some new complaint,
O' which I hae the key, O!

She's had some unco queer mishaps,
Wi' nervish[6] wind and clean collapse,   6nervous
An' naethin' does her guid but draps—
Guid draps o' barley-bree,[7] O!   7whisky

I wouldna care a docken blade,
Gin her accoont she ever paid,
But while she gie'es me a' her trade,
There's ne'er a word o' fee, O!

[8]complaining

[9]whooping-
cough
[10]child's skin
disease

Then De'il hae a' thae girnin[8] wives,
There's ne'er a bairn they hae that thrives,
It's aye the kink-hoast[9] or the hives,[10]
That's gaun to gar them dee, O!

Tak' ony job ye like ava!
Tak' trade, the poopit or the law,
But gin ye're wise, ye'll haud awa
Frae medical degree, O!

Dr David Rorie

The Douglas Tragedy

'Rise up, rise up, now, Lord Douglas,' she says,
    'And put on your armour so bright;
Let it never be said that a daughter of thine
    Was married to a lord under night.

'Rise up, rise up, my seven bold sons,
    And put on your armour so bright,
And take better care of your youngest sister,
    For your eldest's awa the last night.'

He's mounted her on a milk-white steed,
    And himself on a dapple grey,
With a bugelet horn hung down by his side;
    And lightly they rode away.

Lord William lookit o'er his left shoulder,
    To see what he could see,
And there he spy'd her seven brethren bold
    Come riding o'er the lea.

'Light down, light down, Lady Marg'ret,' he said,
  'And hold my steed in your hand,
Until that against your seven brethren bold,
  And your father, I make a stand.'

She held his steed in her milk-white hand
  And never shed one tear,
Until that she saw her seven brethren fa',
  And her father hard fighting, who loved her so
    dear.

'O hold your hand, Lord William!' she said,
  'For your strokes they are wondrous sair;
True lovers I can get many an ane,
  But a father I can never get mair.'

O' she's ta'en out her handkerchief,
  It was o' the holland sae fine,
And aye she dighted[1] her father's bloody wounds,   [1]wiped
  That were redder than the wine.

'O chuse, O chuse, Lady Marg'ret,' he said,
  'O whether will ye gang or bide?'
'I'll gang, I'll gang, Lord William,' she said,
  'For you have left me no other guide.'

He's lifted her on a milk-white steed,
  And himself on a dapple grey,
With a bugelet horn hung down by his side,
  And slowly they baith rade away.

O they rade on, and on they rade,
  And a' by the light of the moon,
Until they came to yon wan water,
  And there they lighted down.

They lighted down to tak a drink
  Of the spring that ran sae clear,
And down the stream ran his gude heart's blood,
  And sair she 'gan to fear.

'Hold up, hold up, Lord William,' she says,
  'For I fear that you are slain!'
''Tis naething but the shadow of my scarlet cloak,
  That shines in the water sae plain.'

O they rade on, and on they rade,
  And a' by the light of the moon,
Until they cam to his mother's ha' door,
  And there they lighted doun.

'Get up, get up, lady mother,' he says,
  'Get up, and let me in!
Get up, get up, lady mother,' he says,
  'For this night my fair lady I've win.

'O mak my bed, lady mother,' he says,
  'O mak it braid and deep!
And lay Lady Marg'ret close at my back,
  And the sounder I will sleep.'

Lord William was dead lang ere midnight,
  Lady Marg'ret lang ere day,
And all true lovers that go thegither,
  May they have mair luck than they!

Lord William was buried in St Marie's kirk,
  Lady Marg'ret in Marie's quire;
Out o' the lady's grave grew a bonny red rose,
  And out o' the knight's a brier.

²entwined And they twa met, and they twa plat,²
  And fain they wad be near;
And a' the warld might ken right weel
  They were twa lovers dear.

But bye and rade the Black Douglas,
  And wow but he was rough!
For he pull'd up the bonny brier,
  And flang 't in St Marie's Loch.

                                        Anon

The Dowie Houms o' Yarrow

Late at e'en, drinkin' the wine,
  Or early in a mornin',
They set a combat them between,
  To fight it in the dawnin'.

'O stay at hame, my noble lord!
  O stay at hame, my marrow!
My cruel brother will you betray,
  On the dowie[1] houms[2] o' Yarrow.'

[1]sad
[2]holms

'O fare ye weel, my lady gaye!
  O fare ye weel, my Sarah!
For I maun gae, tho' I ne'er return
  Frae the dowie banks o' Yarrow.'

She kiss'd his cheek, she kamed his hair,
  As she had done before, O;
She belted on his noble brand,
  An' he's awa to Yarrow.

O he's gane up yon high, high hill—
  I wat he gaed wi' sorrow—
An' in a den spied nine arm'd men,
  I' the dowie houms o' Yarrow.

'O ir[3] ye come to drink the wine,
  As ye hae doon before, O?
Or ir ye come to wield the brand,
  On the bonnie banks o' Yarrow?'

[3]are

'I am no come to drink the wine,
  As I hae done before, O,
But I am come to wield the brand,
  On the dowie houms o' Yarrow.'

Four he hurt, an' five he slew,
  On the dowie houms o' Yarrow,
Till that stubborn knight came him behind,
  An' ran his body thorrow.[4]

[4]through

'Gae hame, gae hame, good-brother John,
    An' tell your sister Sarah
To come an' lift her noble lord,
    Who's sleepin' sound on Yarrow.'

'Yestreen I dream'd a dolefu' dream;
    I ken'd there wad be sorrow;
I dream'd I pu'd the heather green,
    On the dowie banks o' Yarrow.'

She gaed up yon high, high hill—
    I wat she gaed wi sorrow—
An' in a den spy'd nine dead men,
    On the dowie houms o' Yarrow.

She kiss'd his cheek, she kaim'd his hair,
    As oft she did before, O;
She drank the red blood frae him ran,
    On the dowie houms o' Yarrow.

'O haud your tongue, my douchter dear,
    For what needs a' this sorrow?
I'll wed you on a better lord
    Than him you lost on Yarrow.'

'O haud your tongue, my father dear,
    An' dinna grieve your Sarah;
A better lord was never born
    Than him I lost on Yarrow.

⁵oxen 'Tak hame your ousen,[5] take hame your kye,
    For they hae bred our sorrow;
I wiss that they had a' gane mad
    When they cam first to Yarrow.'

                                        Anon

Binnorie

There was twa sisters in a bow'r,
  Binnorie, O Binnorie!
There was twa sisters in a bow'r,
  Binnorie, O Binnorie!
There was twa sisters in a bow'r,
There came a knight to be their wooer.
  By the bonny milldams o' Binnorie.

He courted the eldest wi' glove an ring,
But he lov'd the youngest above a' thing.

He courted the eldest wi' brotch[1] and knife,   [1]brooch
But lov'd the youngest as his life.

The eldest she was vexèd sair,
An' much envi'd her sister fair.

Into her bow'r she could not rest,
Wi' grief an' spite she almos[t] brast.[2]   [2]burst

Upon a morning fair an' clear,
She cried upon her sister dear:

'O sister, come to yon sea stran',
An' see our father's ships come to lan'.'

She's ta'en her by the milk-white han',
An' led her down to yon sea stran'.

The younges[t] stood upon a stane,
The eldest came an' threw her in.

She tooke her by the middle sma',
An' dash'd[3] her bonny back to the jaw.   [3]splash

'O sister, sister, tak my han',
An' I'se mack you heir to a' my lan'.'

89

'O sister, sister, tak my middle,
An' ye's get my goud and my gouden girdle.

'O sister, sister, save my life,
An' I swear I'se never be nae man's wife.'

'Foul fa' the han' that I should tacke,
It twin'd me an' my wardles make.[4]

[4]life's mate

'Your cherry cheeks an' yellow hair
Gars me gae maiden for evermair.'

Sometimes she sank, an' sometimes she swam,
Till she came down yon bonny milldam.

O out it came the miller's son,
An' saw the fair maid swimmin' in.

'O father, father, draw your dam,
Here's either a mermaid or a swan.'

The miller quickly drew the dam,
An' there he found a drown'd woman.

You couldna see her yallow hair
For gold and pearle that were so rare.

You couldna see her middle sma'
For gouden girdle that was sae braw.

You couldna see her fingers white,
For gouden rings that was sae gryte.[5]

[5]great

An' by there came a harper fine,
That harped to the king at dine.

When he did look that lady upon,
He sigh'd and made a heavy moan.

He's ta'en three locks o' her yallow hair,
An' wi' them strung his harp sae fair.

The first tune he did play and sing,
Was, 'Farewell to my father the king.'

The nextin tune that he play'd syne,
Was, 'Farewell to my mother the queen.'

The lasten tune that he play'd then,
  Binnorie, O Binnorie!
Was, 'Wae to my sister, fair Ellen.'
  By the bonnie milldams o' Binnorie.

Anon

Edward, Edward

'Why dois your brand sae drap wi' bluid,
                    Edward, Edward,
Why dois your brand sae drap wi' bluid,
    And why sae sad gang yee O?'
'O I hae killed my hauke sae guid,
                    Mither, mither,
O I hae killed my hauke sae guid,
    And I had nae mair bot hee O.'

'Your haukis bluid was nevir sae reid,
                    Edward, Edward,
Your haukis bluid was nevir sae reid,
    My deir son I tell thee O.'
'O I hae killed my reid-roan steid,
                    Mither, mither,
O I hae killed my reid-roan steid,
    That erst was sae fair and frie O.'

'Your steid was auld, and ye hae gat mair,
                        Edward, Edward,
Your steid was auld, and ye hae gat mair,
¹sorrow   Some other dule[1] ye drie O.'
'O I hae killed my fadir deir,
                        Mither, mither,
O I hae killed my fadir deir,
    Alas, and wae is mee O!'

'And whatten penance wul ye drie for that,
                        Edward, Edward?
And whatten penance wul ye drie for that?
    My deir son, now tell me O.'
'Ile set my feit in yonder boat,
                        Mither, mither,
Ile set my feit in yonder boat,
    And Ile fare ovir the sea O.'

'And what wul ye doe wi' your towirs and your ha',
                        Edward, Edward?
And what wul ye doe wi' your towirs and your ha',
    That were sae fair to see O?'
'Ile let thame stand tul they doun fa',
                        Mither, mither,
Ile let thame stand tul they doun fa',
    For here nevir mair maun I bee O.'

'And what wul ye leive to your bairns and your wife,
                        Edward, Edward?
And what wul ye leive to your bairns and your wife,
    When ye gang ovir the sea O?'
²through   'The warldis room, late them beg thrae[2] life,
                        Mither, mither,
The warldis room, late them beg thrae life,
    For thame nevir mair wul I see O.'

92

'And what wul ye leive to your ain mither deir,
               Edward, Edward?
And what wul ye leive to your ain mither deir?
  My deir son, now tell me O.'
'The curse of hell frae me sall ye beir,
               Mither, mither,
The curse of hell frae me sall ye beir,
  Sic counseils ye gave to me O.'

                        Anon

Fut Like Folk?

Fut like[1] folk in yon braid Buchan lan'?
Folk wha ken their grun like the back o' their han',
Divot and clort[2] and clod, rock, graivel and san'.

Fut like folk in yon gran' Buchan howe?[3]
Folk wha gar[4] their grun near' onything growe,
Neaps and tatties and corn, horse, heifer and yowe.

Fut like folk in yon braw Buchan neuk?[5]
Thrawn-like folk wha ken but the brods o' their
    Beuk,
And Worship the Horseman's Word and the
    shearin heuk.

Folk wha say their say and speir their speir,[6]
Gedder gey birns o'[7] bairns and gey muckle gear,
And gang their ain gait wi' a lach or a spit or a
    sweir.

                  J. C. Milne

[1] what kind of
[2] dirt
[3] plain bounded by hills
[4] make
[5] corner of land
[6] indulge their curiosity
[7] gather a crowd of

The Wife of Usher's Well

There lived a wife at Usher's well,
    And a wealthy wife was she;
She had three stout and stalwart sons,
    And sent them o'er the sea.

They hadna been a week from her,
    A week but barely ane,
When word came to the carline wife
    That her three sons were gane.

They hadna been a week from her,
    A week but barely three,
When word came to the carline wife
    That her sons she'd never see.

'I wish the wind may never cease,
    Nor fashes[1] in the flood,
Till my three sons come hame to me
    In earthly flesh and blood!'

It fell about the Martinmas,
    When nights are lang and mirk,
The carline wife's three sons came hame,
    And their hats were o' the birk.

It neither grew in syke[2] nor ditch,
    Nor yet in ony sheugh;[3]
But at the gates o' Paradise
    That birk grew fair eneugh.

'Blow up the fire, my maidens!
    Bring water from the well!
For a' my house shall feast this night,
    Since my three sons are well.'

And she has made to them a bed,
    She's made it large and wide;
And she's ta'en her mantle her about,
    Sat down at the bedside.

[1] troubles

[2] marsh
[3] ditch

Up then crew the red, red cock,
    And up then crew the gray;
The eldest to the youngest said,
    ''Tis time we were away.'

The cock he hadna craw'd but once,
    And clapp'd his wings at a',
When the youngest to the eldest said,
    'Brother, we must awa.

'The cock doth craw, the day doth daw,
    The channerin'⁴ worm doth chide;   ⁴fretting
Gin we be miss'd out o' our place,
    A sair pain we maun bide.

'Fare ye weel, my mother dear!
    Fareweel to barn and byre!
And fare ye weel, the bonny lass
    That kindles my mother's fire!'

                              Anon

Bonny Kilmeny

Bonny Kilmeny gaed up the glen,
But it wasna to meet Duneira's men,
Nor the rosy monk of the isle to see,
For Kilmeny was pure as pure could be.
It was only to hear the yorlin¹ sing,   ¹yellow-
And pu' the cress-flower round the spring;   hammer
The scarlet hypp and the hindberrye,²   ²raspberry
And the nut that hung frae the hazel tree;
For Kilmeny was pure as pure could be.
But lang may her minny look o'er the wa',
And lang may she seek i' the green-wood shaw;
Lang the laird of Duneira blame,
And lang, lang greet or Kilmeny come hame!

When many a day had come and fled,
When grief grew calm, and hope was dead,
When mass for Kilmeny's soul had been sung,
When the bedes-man had prayed, and the dead
    bell rung,
Late, late in a gloamin' when all was still,
When the fringe was red on the westlin hill,
The wood was sere, the moon i' the wane,
The reek o' the cot hung over the plain,
Like a little wee cloud in the world its lane;
³glowed   When the ingle lowed³ with an eiry leme,⁴
⁴flame   Late, late in the gloamin' Kilmeny came hame!

'Kilmeny, Kilmeny, where have you been?
⁵vale   Lang hae we sought baith holt⁵ and dean;
By linn, by ford, and green-wood tree,
Yet you are halesome and fair to see.
⁶skirt   Where gat you that joup⁶ o' the lile schene?
⁷hair-   That bonny snood⁷ of the birk sae green?
ribbons
And those roses, the fairest that ever were seen?
Kilmeny, Kilmeny, where have you been?'

Kilmeny looked up with a lovely grace,
But nae smile was seen on Kilmeny's face;
As still was her look, and as still was her e'e,
⁸emerald   As the stillness that lay on the emerant⁸ lea,
Or the mist that sleeps on a waveless sea.
For Kilmeny had been she knew not where,
And Kilmeny had seen what she could not declare;
Kilmeny had been where the cock never crew,
Where the rain never fell, and the wind never blew;
But it seemed as the harp of the sky had rung,
And the airs of heaven played round her tongue,
When she spake of the lovely forms she had seen,
And a land where sin had never been;

A land of love, and a land of light,
Withouten sun, or moon, or night,
⁹waved   Where the river swa'd⁹ a living stream,
And the light a pure celestial beam.

The land of vision it would seem,
A still, an everlasting dream. . . .
When seven lang years had come and fled;
When grief was calm, and hope was dead;
When scarce was remembered Kilmeny's name,
Late, late in a gloamin' Kilmeny came hame!

James Hogg

The Rowan

When the days were still as deith
   An' ye couldna see the kye,
Tho' ye'd mebbe hear their breith
   I' the mist oot-by;
When I'd mind the lang grey een
   O' the warlock by the hill,
And sit fleggit, like a wean
   Gin a whaup cried shrill;
Tho' the he'rt wad dee in me
   At a fitstep on the floor,
There was aye the rowan tree
   Wi' its airm across the door.

But that is far, far past,
   And a'thing's just the same,
But there's a whisper up the blast
   O' a dreid I daurna name;
And the shilpit[1] sun is thin   [1]feeble
   As an auld man deein' slow,
And a shade comes creepin' in
   When the fire is fa'in low;
Then I feel the lang een set
   Like a doom upon my heid,
For the warlock's livin yet—
   But the rowan's deid.

Violet Jacob

Bailie Nicol Jarvie

The magistrate took the light out of his servant-maid's hand, and advanced to his scrutiny, like Diogenes in the street of Athens, lantern-in-hand, and probably with as little expectation as that of the cynic, that he was likely to encounter any especial treasure in the course of his researches. The first whom he approached was my mysterious guide, who, seated on a table as I have already described him, with his eyes firmly fixed on the wall, his features arranged into the utmost inflexibility of expression, his hands folded on his breast with an air betwixt carelessness and defiance, his heel patting against the foot of the table, to keep time with the tune which he continued to whistle, submitted to Mr Jarvie's investigation with an air of absolute confidence and assurance, which, for a moment, placed at fault the memory and sagacity of the acute and anxious investigator.

'Ah!—Eh!—Oh!' exclaimed the bailie. 'My conscience!—it's impossible!—and yet—no! Conscience, it canna be!—and yet again—Deil hae me! that I suld say sae—Ye robber—ye cateran[1]—ye born deevil that ye are, to a' bad ends and nae gude ane—can this be you?'

'E'en as ye see, Bailie,' was the laconic answer.

'Conscience! if I am na clean bumbaized[2]—*you*, ye cheat-the-wuddy[3] rogue—*you* here on your venture in the tolbooth[4] o' Glasgow?—What d'ye think's the value o' your head?'

'Uumph!—why, fairly weighed, and Dutch weight, it might weigh down one provost's, four bailies', a town-clerk's, six deacons', besides stentmasters[5]—'

'Ah, ye reiving[6] villain!' interrupted Mr Jarvie. 'But tell ower your sins, and prepare ye, for if I say the word—'

'True, Bailie,' said he who was thus addressed, folding his hands behind him with the utmost *nonchalance*, 'but ye will never say that word.'

---

[1]freebooter   [2]confounded   [3]gallows
[4]gaol   [5]assessors   [6]thieving

'And why suld I not, sir?' exclaimed the magistrate,—
'why suld I not? Answer me that,—why suld I not?'

'For three sufficient reasons, Bailie Jarvie: First, for auld
langsyne; second, for the sake of the auld wife ayont the
fire at Stuckavrallachan, that made some mixture of our
bluids, to my own proper shame be it spoken! that has a
cousin wi' accounts, and yarn winnles,[7] and looms, and
shuttles, like a mere mechanical person; and lastly, Bailie,
because if I saw a sign o' your betraying me, I would
plaster that wa' with your harns[8] ere the hand of man
could rescue you!'

'Ye're a bauld, desperate villain, sir,' retorted the un-
daunted Bailie; 'and ye ken that I ken ye to be sae, and
that I wadna stand a moment for may ain risk.'

'I ken weel,' said the other, 'ye hae gentle bluid in
your veins, and I wad be laith to hurt my ain kinsman.
But I'll gang out here as free as I came in, or the very
wa's o' Glasgow tolbooth shall tell o't these ten years to
come.'

'Weel, weel,' said Mr Jarvie, 'bluid's thicker than water;
and it liesna in kith, kin, and ally, to seek motes in ilk
other's een if other een see them no. It wad be sair news
to the auld wife below the Ben of Stuckavrallachan, that
you, ye Hieland limmer,[9] had knockit out my harns,[10] or
that I had kilted[11] you up in a tow.[12] But ye'll own, ye
dour deevil, that were it no your very sell, I wad hae
grippit the best man in the Hielands.'

'Ye wad hae tried, Cousin,' answered my guide, 'that I
wot weel; but I doubt ye wad hae come aff wi' the short
measure; for we gang-there-out[13] Hieland bodies are an
unchancy[14] generation when you speak to us o' bondage.
We downa bide the coercion of gude braid claith about
our hinderlans, let a be[15] breeks o' freestone, and garters o'
iron.'

'Ye'll find the stane breeks and the airn garters—ay,
and the hemp cravat, for a' that, neighbour,' replied the
Bailie. 'Nae man in a civilized country ever played the

---

[7]winders	[8]brains	[9]rascal
[10]brains	[11]tucked	[12]rope
[13]out-of-doors	[14]risky	[15]not to mention

pliskies[16] ye hae done—But e'en pickle in your ain pock-neuk[17]—I hae gi'en ye warning.'

'Well, Cousin,' said the other, 'ye'll wear black at my burial?'

'Deil a black cloak will be there, Robin, but the corbies[18] and the hoodie-craws, I'se gie ye my hand on that. But whar's the gude thousand pund Scots that I lent ye, man, and when am I to see it again?'

'Where it is,' replied my guide, after the affectation of considering for a moment, 'I cannot justly tell—probably where last year's snaw is.'

'And that's on the tap of Schehallion, ye Hieland dog,' said Mr Jarvie; 'and I look for payment frae you where ye stand.'

'Ay,' replied the Highlander, 'but I keep neither snaw nor dollars in my sporran. And as to when you'll see it —why, just when the king enjoys his ain again, as the auld sang says.'

'Warst of a', Robin,' retorted the Glaswegian,—'I mean, ye disloyal traitor. Warst of a'!—Wad ye bring popery in on us, and arbitrary power, and a foist and a warming-pan, and the set forms, and the curates, and the auld enormities o' surplices and cearments? Ye had better stick to your auld trade o' theft-boot, black-mail, spreaghs,[19] and gill-ravaging[20]—better stealing nowte than ruining nations.'

When, however, I recollected the circumstances in which we formerly met, I could not doubt that the billet was most probably designed for him. He had made a marked figure among those mysterious personages over whom Diana seemed to exercise an influence, and from whom she experienced an influence in her turn. It was painful to think that the fate of a being so amiable was involved in that of desperadoes of this man's description; yet it seemed impossible to doubt it. Of what use, however, could this person be to my father's affairs?—I could think only of one. Rashleigh Osbaldistone had, at the instigation of

[16]pranks   [17]depend on yourself   [18]carrion-crows
[19]cattle-lifting   [20]depredation

Miss Vernon, certainly found means to produce Mr Campbell when his presence was necessary to exculpate me from Morris's accusation. Was it not possible that her influence, in like manner, might prevail on Campbell to produce Rashleigh? Speaking on this supposition, I requested to know where my dangerous kinsman was, and when Mr Campbell had seen him. The answer was indirect.

'It's a kittle cast[21] she has gien me to play; but yet it's fair play, and I winna baulk her. Mr Osbaldistone, I dwell not very far from hence – my kinsman can show you the way. Leave Mr Owen to do the best he can in Glasgow,— do you come and see me in the glens, and it's like I may pleasure you, and stead your father in his extremity. I am but a poor man; but wit's better than wealth. And, cousin,' (turning from me to address Mr Jarvie) 'if he daur venture sae muckle as to eat a dish of Scotch collops, and a leg o' red-deer venison wi' me, come ye wi' this Sassenach gentleman as far as Drymen or Bucklivie, or the Clachan[22] of Aberfoil will be better than ony o' them, and I'll hae somebody waiting to weise[23] ye the gate to the place where I may be for the time. What say ye, man? There's my thumb, I'll ne'er beguile thee.'

'Na, na, Robin,' said the cautious burgher, 'I seldom like to leave the Gorbals; I have nae freedom to gang amang your wild hills, Robin, and your kilted red-shanks, it disna become my place, man.'

'The devil damn your place and you baith!' reiterated Campbell. 'The only drap o' gentle bluid that's in your body was our great granduncle's that was justified[24] at Dumbarton, and you set yourself up to say ye wad derogate frae your place to visit me! Hark thee, man—I owe thee a day in harst—I'll pay up your thousan pund Scots, plack and bawbee, gin ye'll be an honest fallow for anes, and just daiker[25] up the gate wi' this Sassenach.'

'Hout awa' wi' your gentility,' replied the Bailie; 'carry your gentle bluid to the Cross, and see what ye'll buy wi't.

[21]ticklish part   [22]hamlet
[23]direct   [24]executed
[25]stroll

But, if I *were* to come, wad ye really and soothfastly pay me the siller?'

'I swear to ye,' said the Highlander, 'upon the halidome[26] of him that sleeps beneath the grey stane at Inch-Cailleach.'

'Say nae mair, Robin—say nae mair—We'll see what may be dune. But ye maunna expect me to gang ower the Highland line—I'll gae beyond the line at no rate. Ye maun meet me about Bucklivie or the Clachan of Aberfoil, and dinna forget the needful.

'Ochon, that I sud ever be concerned in aiding and abetting an escape frae justice! It will be a shame and disgrace to me and mine, and my very father's memory, for ever.'

'Hout tout, man! let that flee stick in the wa',' answered his kinsman; 'when the dirt's dry it will rub out—Your father, honest man, could look ower a friend's fault as weel as anither.'

'Ye may be right, Robin,' replied the Bailie, after a moment's reflection; 'he was a considerate man the deacon; he ken'd we had a' our frailties, and he lo'ed his friends—Ye'll no hae forgotten him, Robin?' This question he put in a softened tone, conveying as much at least of the ludicrous as the pathetic.

'Forgotten him!' replied the kinsman—'what suld ail me to forget him?—a wapping[27] weaver he was, and wrought my first pair o' hose.—But come awa' kinsman,

'Come fill up my cup, come fill up my cann,
Come saddle my horses, and call up my man;
Come open your gates, and let me gae free,
I daurna stay langer in bonny Dundee.'

'Whisht, sir!' said the magistrate, in an authoritative tone—'lilting and singing sae near the latter end o' the Sabbath! This house may hear ye sing anither tune yet—Aweel, we hae a' backslidings to answer for—Stanchells, open the door.'

The jailor obeyed, and we all sallied forth. Stanchells looked with some surprise at the two strangers, wondering,

26sanctity   27stout

102

doubtless, how they came into these premises without his knowledge; but Mr Jarvie's 'Friends o' mine, Stanchells—friends o' mine,' silenced all disposition to inquiries. We now descended into the lower vestibule, and hallooed more than once for Dougal, to which summons no answer was returned; when Campbell observed, with a sardonic smile, 'That if Dougal was the lad he kent him, he would scarce wait to get thanks for his ain share of the night's wark, but was in all probability on the full trot to the pass of Ballamaha'—

'And left us—and abune a', me, mysell, locked up in the tolbooth, a' night!' exclaimed the Bailie, in ire and perturbation. 'Ca' for forehammers, sledge-hammers, pinches and coulters; send for Deacon Yettlin, the smith, and let him ken that Bailie Jarvie's shut up in the tolbooth by a Hieland blackguard, whom he'll hang up as high as Haman'—

'When ye catch him,' said Campbell, gravely; 'but stay—the door is surely not locked.'

Indeed, on examination, we found that the door was not only left open, but that Dougal in his retreat had, by carrying off the keys along with him, taken care than no one should exercise his office of porter in a hurry.

'He has glimmerings o' common sense now, that creature Dougal,' said Campbell;—'he ken'd an open door might hae served me at a pinch.'

We were by this time in the street.

'I tell you, Robin,' said the magistrate, 'in my puir mind, if ye live the life ye do, ye suld hae ane o' your gillies door-keeper in every jail in Scotland, in case o' the warst.'

'Ane o' my kinsmen a bailie in ilka burgh will just do as weel, cousin Nicol—So, gude-night or gude-morning to ye; and forget not the Clachan of Aberfoil.'

And without waiting for an answer, he sprang to the other side of the street, and was lost in darkness. Immediately on his disappearance, we heard him give a low whistle of peculiar modulation, which was instantly replied to.

'Hear to the Hieland deevils,' said Mr Jarvie; 'they think themselves on the skirts of Benlomond already,

where they may gang whewing[28] and whistling about
without minding Sunday or Saturday.' Here he was
interrupted by something which fell with a heavy clash on
the street before us—'Gude guide us! what's this mair o't?
—Mattie, haud up the lantern—Conscience! if it isna the
keys!—Well, that's just as weel—they cost the burgh
siller, and there might hae been some clavers[29] about the
loss o' them. O, an Bailie Grahame were to get word o'
this night's job, it wad be a sair hair in my neck!'

As we were still but a few steps from the tolbooth door,
we carried back these implements of office, and consigned
them to the head jailor, who, in lieu of the usual mode of
making good his post by turning the keys, was keeping
sentry in the vestibule till the arrival of some assistant,
whom he had summoned in order to replace the Celtic
fugitive Dougal.

Having discharged this piece of duty to the burgh, and
my road lying the same way with the honest magistrate's,
I profited by the light of his lantern, and he by my arm,
to find our way through the streets, which, whatever they
may now be, were then dark, uneven, and ill-paved. Age
is easily propitiated by attentions from the young. The
Bailie expressed himself interested in me, and added,
'That since I was nane o' that play-acting and play-
ganging generation, whom his saul hated, he wad be glad
if I wad eat a reisted[30] haddock, or a fresh herring, at
breakfast wi' him the morn, and meet my friend, Mr Owen,
whom, by that time, he would place at liberty.'

'My dear sir,' said I, when I had accepted of the invi-
tation with thanks, 'how could you possibly connect me
with the stage?'

'I watna,' replied Mr Jarvie;—'it was a bletherin'[31]
phrasin' chield they ca' Fairservice, that cam at e'en to get
an order to send the crier through the toun for ye at
skreigh o' day the morn. He tell't me whae ye were, and
how ye were sent frae your father's house because ye
wadna be a dealer, and that ye mightna disgrace your
family wi' ganging on the stage. Ane Hammorgaw, our

[28]crying   [29]chatter
[30]dried   [31]glib

104

precentor, brought him here, and said he was an auld acquaintance; but I sent them baith awa' wi' a flae[32] in their lug for bringing me sic an errand on sic a night. But I see he's a fule-creature a'thegither, and clean mista'en about ye. I like ye, man,' he continued; 'I like a lad that will stand by his friends in trouble—I aye did it myself, and sae did the deacon my father, rest and bless him! But ye suldna keep ower muckle company wi' Hielandmen and thae wild cattle. Can a man touch pitch and no be defiled?—aye mind that. Nae doubt, the best and wisest may err—Once, twice, and thrice, have I backslidden, man, and dune three things this night—my father wadna hae believed his een if he could hae looked up and seen me do them.'

He was by this time arrived at the door of his own dwelling. He paused, however, on the threshold, and went on in a solemn tone of deep contrition,—'Firstly, I hae thought my ain thoughts on the Sabbath—secondly, I hae gi'en security for an Englishman, and, in the third and last place, well-a-day! I hae let an ill-doer escape from the place of imprisonment—But there's balm in Gilead, Mr Osbaldistone—Mattie, I can let mysell in— see Mr Osbaldistone to Luckie Flyter's at the corner o' the wynd.—Mr Osbaldistone'—in a whisper—'ye'll offer nae incivility to Mattie—she's an honest man's daughter, and a near cousin o' the Laird o' Limmerfield's.'

Sir Walter Scott

[32]flea

The Pawky Duke

[1]trickery

There aince was a very pawky duke,
    Far kent for his joukery-pawkery,[1]
Wha owned a hoose wi' a gran outlook,
    A gairden an' a rockery,
Hech mon! The pawky duke!
    Hoot aye! An a' rockery!
For a bonnet laird[2] wi' a sma' kailyaird,
    Is naethin' but a mockery.

[2]one whose
farm is his
own property

He dwalt far up a Heelant glen
    Where the foamin' flood an' the crag is,
He dined each day on the usquebae[3]
    An' he washed it doon wi' haggis.
Hech mon! The pawky duke!
    Hoots aye! An' a haggis!
For that's the way that the Heelanters dae
    Whaur the foamin' flood an' the crag is.

[3]whisky

He wore a sporran an' a dirk,
    An' a beard like besom bristles,
He was an elder o' the kirk,
    And he hated kists o' whistles.[4]
Hech mon! The pawky duke!
    An' doon on kists o' whistles!
They're a' reid-heidit fowk up North,
    Wi' beards like besom bristles.

[4]organs

His hair was reid as ony rose,
    His legs was lang an' bony,
He keepit a hoast[5] an' a rubbin'-post,
    An' a buskit cockernony.[6]
Hech mon! The pawky duke!
    An' a buskit cockernony!
Ye ne'er will ken true Heelantmen
    Wha'll own they hadna ony.

[5]cough
[6]hair bound
up in a snood

Syne ilka fowre hoors through the day
    He took a muckle jorum,
An' when the gloamin' gaither'd grey
    Got fou wi' great decorum.
Hech mon! The pawky duke!
    Blin' fou wi' great decorum!
There ne'er were males amang the Gaels
    But lo'ed a muckle jorum.

An' if he met a Sassenach,
    Attour in Caledonia,
He gart him lilt in a cotton kilt
    Till he took an acute pneumonia.
Hech mon! The pawky duke!
    An' a Sassenach wi' pneumonia!
He lat him feel that the Land o' the Leal
    'S nae far frae Caledonia.

Then aye afore he socht his bed
    He danced the Gillie Callum,
An wi's Kilmarnock owre his neb,
    What evil could befall him?
Hech mon! The pawky duke!
    What evil could befall him?
When he cast his buits an' soopled his cuits
    Wi' a gude-gaun Gillie Callum.

But they brocht a joke, they did indeed,
    Ae day for his eedification,
An' they needed to trephine his heid,
    Sae he deed o' the operation.
Hech mon! The pawky duke!
    Wae's me for the operation!
For weel I wot this typical Scot
    Was a michty loss to the nation.

Dr David Rorie

A Whigmaleerie

There was an Auchtergaven mouse
(I canna mind his name)

Wha met in wi' a hirplin¹ louse,
Sair trauchl'd² for her hame.

'My friend, I'm hippit,³ and nae doot,
Ye'll heist⁴ me on my wey'.
The mouse but squinted doun his snoot,
And wi' a breenge was by.

Or lang he cam to his ain door,

Doun be a condie-hole;⁵
And thocht, as he was stappin owre;
Vermin are ill to thole.

William Soutar

Crowdieknowe

Oh to be at Crowdieknowe,
When the last trump blaws,

An' see the deid come loupin'¹ owre
The auld grey wa's.

Muckle men wi' tousled beards,

I grat² at as a bairn,
'll scramble frae the croodit clay

Wi' feck³ o' swearin'.

An' glower⁴ at God an' a' his gang
O' angels i' the lift,
Thae trashy bleezin' French-like folk
Wha gar'd them shift!

Fain the weemun-folk'll seek
To mak' them haud their row,

Fegs,⁵ God's no blate⁶ gin he stirs up
The men o' Crowdieknowe!

Hugh MacDiarmid

The Flowers of the Forest

I've heard them lilting at our yowe-milking—
    Lasses a-lilting before dawn of day;
But now they are moaning on ilka green loaning—
    The Flowers of the Forest are a' wede away.

At buchts,[1] in the morning, nae blythe lads are
    scorning;   [1]folds
    Lasses are lonely and dowie and wae;—
Nae daffin',[2] nae gabbin'—but sighing and
    sabbing,   [2]dalliance
    Ilk ane lifts her leglin[3] and hies her away.   [3]milk-pail

In hairst, at the shearing, nae youths now are
    jeering—
    Bandsters are runkled and lyart[4] or grey: [4]hoary
At fair or at preaching, nae wooing, nae
    fleeching—
    The Flowers of the Forest are a' wede away.

At e'en, in the gloaming, nae swankies[5] are roam-
    ing,   [5]swains
    'Bout stacks with the lasses at bogle[6] to play;   [6]hide-and-
But ilk maid sits drearie, lamenting her dearie—   seek
    The Flowers of the Forest are a' wede away.

Dool and wae for the order sent our lads to the
    Border!
    The English, for ance, by guile wan the day;—
The Flowers of the Forest, that foucht aye the
    foremost—
    The prime of our land—are cauld in the clay.

We'll hear nae mair lilting at the yowe-milking;
    Women and bairns are heartless and wae,
Sighing and moaning on ilka green loaning—
    The Flowers of the Forest are a' wede away.

Jane Elliot

Annals of the Parish

The Placing of Mr Balwhidder

First of the placing.—It was a great affair, for I was put in by the patron, and the people knew nothing whatsoever of me, and their hearts were stirred into strife on the occasion, and they did all that lay within the compass of their power to keep me out, insomuch that there was obliged to be a guard of soldiers to protect the presbytery; and it was a thing that made my heart grieve when I heard the drum beating and the fife playing as we were going to the kirk. The people were really mad and vicious, and flung dirt upon us as we passed, and reviled us all, and held out the finger of scorn at me; but I endured it with a resigned spirit, compassionating their wilfulness and blindness. Poor old Mr Kilfuddy of the Braehill got such a clash of glar[1] on the side of his face that his eye was almost extinguished.

When we got to the kirk door it was found to be nailed up, so as by no possibility to be opened. The sergeant of the soldiers wanted to break it; but I was afraid that the heritors would grudge and complain of the expense of a new door, and I supplicated him to let it be as it was. We were, therefore, obligated to go in by a window, and the crowd followed us in the most unreverent manner, making the Lord's house like an inn on a fair day with their grievous yellyhooing. During the time of the psalm and the sermon they behaved themselves better; but when the induction came on their clamour was dreadful, and Thomas Thorl, the weaver, a pious zealot in that time, got up and protested, and said, 'Verily, verily, I say into you, he that entereth not by the door into the sheepfold, but climbeth up some other way, the same is a thief and a robber.' And I thought I would have a hard and sore time of it with such an out-strapolous[2] people. Mr Given, that was then the minister of Lugton, was a jocose man, and would have his joke even at a solemnity. When the

[1] splatter of mud
[2] unruly

laying of the hands upon me was adoing, he could not get near enough to put on his, but he stretched out his staff and touched my head, and said, to the great diversion of the rest, 'This will do well enough; timber to timber;' but it was an unfriendly saying of Mr Given, considering the time and the place, and the temper of my people.

After the ceremony, we then got out at the window, and it was a heavy day to me; but we went to the manse, and there we had an excellent dinner, which Mrs Watts of the new inns of Irville prepared at my request and sent her chaise-driver to serve (for he was likewise her waiter, she having then but one chaise, and that no often called for).

But, although my people received me in this unruly manner, I was resolved to cultivate civility among them, and, therefore, the very next morning I began a round of visitations; but, oh! it was a steep brae that I had to climb and it needed a stout heart. For I found the doors in some places barred against me; in others, the bairns, when they saw me coming, ran crying to their mothers, 'Here's the feckless Mess-John³!' and then, when I went into the houses, their parents wouldna ask me to sit down, but with a scornful way said, 'Honest man, what's your pleasure here?' Nevertheless, I walked about from door to door like a dejected beggar till I got the almous deed of a civil reception,—and (who would have thought it?) from no less a person than the same Thomas Thorl that was so bitter against me in the kirk on the foregoing day.

Thomas was standing at the door with his green duffle⁴ apron, and his red Kilmarnock nightcap,—I mind him as well as if it was but yesterday—and he had seen me going from house to house, and in what manner I was rejected; and his bowels were moved, and he said to me in a kind manner:

'Come in, sir, and ease yoursel': this will never do: the clergy are God's gorbies,⁵ and for their Master's sake it behoves us to respect them. There was no ane in the whole parish mair against you than mysel'; but this early visitation

³nickname for a Minister
⁴a coarse woollen cloth
⁵ravens

is a symptom of grace that I couldna have expectit from a bird out the nest of patronage.'

I thanked Thomas, and went in with him, and we had some solid conversation together. I told him that it was not so much the pastor's duty to feed the flock as to herd them well; and that, although there might be some abler with the head than me, there wasna a he within the bounds of Scotland more willing to waṭch the fold by night and by day. And Thomas said he had not heard a mair sound observe for some time, and that, if I held to that doctrine in the poopit, it wouldna be long till I would work a change.

'I was mindit,' quoth he, 'never to set my foot within the kirk door while you were there; but to testify, and no to condemn without a trial, I'll be there next Lord's day, and egg my neighbours to be likewise: so ye'll no have to preach to the bare walls and the laird's family.'

The Second Mrs Balwhidder

Soon after this, the time was drawing near for my second marriage. I had placed my affections, with due consideration, on Miss Lizy Kibbock, the well-brought-up daughter of Mr Joseph Kibbock of the Gorbyholm, who was the first that made a speculation in the farming way in Ayrshire, and whose cheese were of such an excellent quality that they have, under the name of Delap-cheese, spread far and wide over the civilized world. Miss Lizy and I were married on the 29th day of April (with some inconvenience on both sides) on account of the dread that we had of being married in May; for it is said,

'Of the marriages in May,
The bairns die of a decay.'

However, married we were, and we hired the Irville chaise, and with Miss Jenny her sister, and Becky Cairns her niece, who sat on a portmanty at our feet, we went on a pleasure jaunt to Glasgow, where we bought a miracle of useful things for the manse that neither the first Mrs Balwhidder nor me had ever thought of: the second Mrs

Balwhidder that was had a geni for management, and it was extraordinary what she could go through. Well may I speak of her with commendations; for she was the bee that made my honey, although at first things did not go so clear with us. For she found the manse rookit and herrit, and there was such a supply of plenishing of all sort wanted that I thought myself ruined and undone by her care and industry. There was such a buying of wool to make blankets, with a booming of the meikle wheel to spin the same, and such birring of the little wheel for sheets and napery, that the manse was for many a day like an organ kist. Then we had milk cows, and the calves to bring up, and a kirning of butter, and a making of cheese; in short, I was almost by myself with the jangle and din, which prevented me from writing a book as I had proposed. And for a time I thought of the peaceful and kindly nature of the first Mrs Balwhidder with a sigh; but the outcoming was soon manifest. The second Mrs Balwhidder sent her butter on the market-days to Irville and her cheese from time to time to Glasgow—to Mrs Firlot, that kept the huxtry[6] in the Saltmarket—; and they were both so well made that our dairy was just a coining of money, insomuch that, after the first year, we had the whole tot of my stipend to put untouched into the bank.

Tea-drinking

Before this year, the drinking of tea was little known in the parish, saving among a few of the heritors' houses on a Sabbath evening; but now it became very rife. Yet the commoner sort did not like to let it be known that they were taking to the new luxury, especially the elderly women, who, for that reason, had their ploys in out-houses and by-places, just as the witches lang syne had their sinful possets and galravitchings;[7] and they made their tea for common in the pint-stoup,[8] and drank it out of caps and luggies,[9] for there were but few among them that had cups and saucers. Well do I remember that, one

[6]general shop   [7]drinkings and riotous meetings
[8]two-quart measure   [9]wooden bowls

night in harvest, in this very year, as I was taking my twilight dauner aneath the hedge along the back side of Thomas Thorl's yard, meditating on the goodness of Providence, and looking at the sheaves of victual on the field, I heard his wife, and two three other carlins, with their Bohea in the inside of the hedge; and no doubt but it had a lacing of the conek,[10] for they were all cracking like pen-guns. But I gave them a sign, by a loud host, that Providence sees all, and it skailed the bike,[11] for I heard them, like guilty creatures, whispering, and gathering up their truck-pots[12] and trenchers,[13] and cowering away home.

And here I am bound in truth to say that, although I never could abide the smuggling, both on its own account, and for the evils that grew therefrom to the country side, I lost some of my dislike to the tea after Mrs Malcolm began to traffic in it, and we then had it for our breakfast in the morning at the manse, as well as in the afternoon. But what I thought most of it for was that it did no harm to the head of the drinkers—which was not always the case with the possets that were in fashion before. There is no meeting now in the summer evenings, as I remember often happened in my younger days, with decent ladies coming home with red faces, tosy and cosh,[14] from a posset-masking. So, both from its temperance and on account of Mrs Malcolm's sale, I refrained from the November in this year to preach against tea; but I never lifted the weight of my displeasure from off the smuggling trade, until it was utterly put down by the strong hand of government.

Tea-smuggling

Shortly after the revival of the smuggling, an exciseman was put among us. The first was Robin Bicker, a very civil lad that had been a flunkey with Sir Hugh Montgomerie, when he was a residenter in Edinburgh, before the old Sir

[10]brandy [11]spilled the hive
[12]teapots [13]plates
[14]tipsy, pleased with themselves

Hugh's death. He was a queer fellow, and had a coothy way of getting in about folk, the which was very serviceable to him in his vocation. Nor was he overly gleg:[15] but when a job was ill done, and he was obliged to notice it, he would often break out on the smugglers for being so stupid; so that for an excisemen he was wonderfully well liked, and did not object to a waught of brandy at a time, when the auld wives ca'd it well-water. It happened, however, that some unneighbourly person sent him notice of a clecking[16] of tea-chests, or brandy kegs, at which both Jenny and Betty Pawkie were the howdies;[17] and Robin could not but enter their house. However, before going in, he just cried at the door to somebody on the road, so as to let the twa industrious lasses hear he was at hand. They were not slack in closing the trance-door,[18] and putting stoups and stools behind it, so as to cause trouble, and give time before anybody could get in. They then emptied their chaff-bed, and filled the tikeing with tea, and Betty went in on the top, covering herself with the blanket, and graining like a woman in labour. It was thought that Robin Bicker himself would not have been overly particular in searching the house, considering there was a woman seemingly in the dead-thraws; but a sorner,[19] an incomer from the east country, that hung about the change-house as a divor hostler,[20] and would rather gang a day's journey in the dark, than turn a spade in daylight, came to him as he stood at the door, and went in with him to see the sport. Robin, for some reason, could not bid him go away, and both Betty and Janet were sure he was in the plot against them. Indeed, it was always thought he was an informer; and no doubt he was something not canny, for he had a down look.

It was some time before the doorway was cleared of the stoups and stools; and Jenny was in great concern, and flustered, as she said, for her poor sister, who was taken with a heart-colic. 'I'm sorry for her,' said Robin; 'but I'll be as quiet as possible.' And so he searched all the house,

---

[15]too observant
[16]nestful
[17]midwives
[18]door between outer door and kitchen
[19]sponger
[20]picking up chance jobs

but found nothing; at the which his companion, the divor east-country hostler, swore an oath that could not be misunderstood. Without more ado, but, as all thought, against the grain, Robin went up to sympathise with Betty in the bed, whose groans were loud and vehement. 'Let me feel your pulse,' said Robin; and he looted[21] down as she put forth her arm from aneath the clothes, and, laying his hand on the bed, cried, 'Hey! what's this? This is a costly filling.' Upon which Betty jumpet up quite recovered, and Jenny fell to the wailing and railing; while the hostler from the east country took the bed of tea on his back, to carry it to the change-house, till a cart was gotten to take it into the custom-house at Irville.

Betty Pawkie, being thus suddenly cured, and grudging the loss of property, took a knife in her hand, and, as the divor was crossing the burn at the stepping-stones that lead to the back of the change-house, she ran after him and ripped up the tikeing, and sent all the tea floating away on the burn. And this was thought a brave action of Betty, and the story not a little helped to lighten our melancholy meditations.

A Penny Wedding

But I was now growing old, and could go seldomer out among my people than in former days; so that I was less a partaker of their ploys and banquets, either at birth, bridal, or burial. I heard, however, all that went on at them, and I made it a rule, after giving the blessing at the end of the ceremony, to admonish the bride and bridegroom to ca' canny, and join trembling with their mirth. It behoved me on one occasion, however, to break through a rule that age and frailty imposed upon me, and to go to the wedding of Tibby Banes, the daughter of the betherel,[22] for she had once been a servant in the manse, besides the obligation upon me from her father's part, both in the kirk and kirkyard. Mrs Balwhidder went with me, for she liked to countenance the pleasantries of my

[21]bent
[22]beadle

people; and, over and above all, it was a pay-wedding[23] in order to set up the bridegroom in a shop.

There was, to be sure, a great multitude, gentle and semple, of all denominations, with two fiddles and a bass, and the volunteers' fife and drum; and the jollity that went on was a perfect feast of itself, though the wedding-supper was a prodigy of abundance. The auld carles kecklet with fainness[24] as they saw the young dancers, and the carlins sat on forms as mim[25] as May puddocks with their shawls pinned apart to show their muslin napkins. But after supper, when they had got a glass of the punch, their heels showed their mettle, and grannies danced with their oyes,[26] holding out their hands as if they had been spinning with two rocks. I told Colin Mavis, the poet, that an *Infare*[27] was a fine subject for his muse, and soon after he indited an excellent ballad under that title, which he projects to publish, with other ditties, by subscription; and I have no doubt a liberal and discerning public will give him all manner of encouragement, for that is the food of talent of every kind, and without cheering no one can say what an author's faculty naturally is.

John Galt

[23]where guests paid
[25]demure
[27]wedding feast
[24]chuckled with pleasure
[26]grand-children

Pride

Did iver ye see the like o' that?
¹wonder   The warld's fair fashioned to winder[1] at!
Heuch—dinna tell me! Yon's Fishie Pete
That cried the haddies in Ferry Street
Set up wi' his coats an' his grand cigars
In ane o' thae stinkin' motor-cars!

I mind the time (an' it's no far past)
When he wasna for fleein' alang sae fast,
An' doon i' the causey his cairt wad stand
As he roared oot 'Haddies!' below his hand;
Ye'd up wi' yer windy an' doon he'd loup
²croup   Frae the shaft o' the cairt by the sheltie's doup.[2]

Ay, muckle cheenges an' little sense,
A bawbee's wit an' a poond's pretence!
For there's him noo wi' his neb to the sky,
³swung,   I' yon deil's machinery swiggit[3] by,
whirled   An' me, that whiles gied him a piece to eat,
Tramps aye to the kirk on my ain twa feet.

And neebours, mind ye, the warld's agley
Or we couldna see what we've seen the day;
Guid fortune's blate whaur she's weel desairv't
The sinner fu' and the godly stairv't,
An' fowk like me an' my auld guidman
Jist wearied daein' the best we can!

I've kept my lips an' my tongue frae guile
An' kept mysel' to mysel' the while;
Agin a' wastrels I've aye been set
An I'm no for seekin' to thole them yet;
A grand example I've been through life,
A righteous liver, a thrifty wife.

But oh! the hert o' a body bleeds,
⁴spilt   For favours sclarried[4] on sinfu' heids.
Wait you a while! Ye needna think
They'll no gang frae him wi' cairds an' drink!
They'll bring nae blessin', they winna bide,
For the warst sin, neebours, is pride, aye, pride!

                                            Violet Jacob

The Auld House

There's a puckle[1] lairds in the auld house   [1] a good few
wha haud the waas thegither:
there's no muckle graith[2] in the auld house   [2] furniture
nor smeddum[3] aither.   [3] mettle

It was aince a braw and bauld house
and guid for onie weather,
kings and lords thranged in the auld house
or[4] it gaed a'smither.[5]   [4] before
     [5] to pieces

There were kings and lords in the auld house
and birds o monie a feather:
there were sangs and swords in the auld house
that rattled ane anither.

It was aince a braw and bauld house
and guid for onie weather:
but it's noo a scruntit[6] and cauld house   [6] stunted
whaur lairdies forgaither.

Lat's caa in the folk to the auld house,
the puir folk aa thegither;
it's sunkit on rock is the auld house,
and the rock's their brither.

It was aince a braw and bauld house
and guid for onie weather:
but the folk maun funder[7] the auld house   [7] put asunder
and bigg[8] up anither.   [8] build

William Soutar

Daith an' the Gang'ril

Me in a consecrated grave,
The pauper's undisputed richt,
Weel doon amang the crumblin' lave,
Whaur day's a' yin wi' en'less nicht.

Yon trashy coffin could'na aye
Resist the siege o' earth an' stanes,
Sae sax-month saw the lid gi'e wey,
An' a'-thing dribblin ow're ma banes.

An antran maggot here and there
Can a'-maist send a body mad
Chowin' its wey throu' skin an' hair
As heedlessly the he'rtless wad.

O Consciousness, desert ye'r trust
An' brak wi' a' that instance ocht
Or come ye legions frae the dust,
An' nullify ma ev'ry thocht.

But listenin' whaun there's nocht tae hear,
An' lookin' whaun there's less tae see,
An' no' gaun gyte within the 'ear
Says something for ma sanity.

Fouk tramplin' ow're the grass abuin,
Maun read their fate on ilka stane,
Syne doon they come whiles unco suin,
The landlord's heir, the tinker's wean.

Ae welcome blink as yin computes
This wae-fu' warl ane'th the swaird.
Gin Daith descends on man's pursuits
What's for the gang'ril's for the Laird.

But this is no ma hin'-maist state
Wi' soull an' body pairtit sae,
The trumpet ca' sall end their wait,
An' bind them in Eternity.

T. T. Kilbucho

Lintie in a Cage

The poet Furgusson in Darien madhouse, Edinburgh, 1774.
His attendant speaks.

Yon is the laddie lo'ed to daunder far
Whaur the burnie bickers by the Hermitage
That sits at the fit o Braid; or whaur Dunbar,
Reid as its rocks, breists the blae[1] Frith's blawn   [1]blue
    rage.
Noo, in this waefu den
Mang puir wit-wandered men,
His wandering wits aye sing.
I mind my grannie's owercome, 'Even in a cage
Lintics maun sing.'

I dinna ken the richts o it: he tummelt doun
(Or so the clash[2] goes) a fell turnpike stair,   [2]gossip
Aiblins[3] a wheen the waur o drink, the stoun   [3]perhaps
Whummelt his harns:[4] noo, as ye see, sits there,   [4]brains
Frae his bedding strae[5] a croun   [5]straw
Tae set his broo abune,
Plaiting wi muckle care,
'Crouned or uncrouned' said my grannie, dovering,[6]   [6]dozing
'The makar's aye a king.'

He's aye read-readin his Bibles: whiles will rail
Against the miscreant (whilk he swears he kens)
That into oor Lord's body drave the nails.
Guid-sakes! He thinks him amang leevin men!
It scunners me tae hear,
Yet aiblins it's no that queer.
As Innocence suffered then,
Sinsyne maun the saikless thole[7] frae cruel men   [7]innocent
Their share o yon suffering.   suffer

Whiles he havers o his pet starling, an' hoo there
    crept
Doun the chimley-breist, aince, in the pit-mirk
    nicht,
A lean cat, huntin-hungered, that stalked, an'
    leapt
On the fleggit bird, whase maister wauk tae its
    fricht
O cheepings an' flichterings,
⁸blood-soiled Ower late for the bluid-clarted[8] wings
Sae savaged the while he slept.
'Aye, e'en i' the bield o the hearth will the black
    Fate spring,'
⁹old woman Quo' cummer,[9] 'on the cherished wings.'

I ken ye maun wark for their guid agin their will,
¹⁰daft Thae doited[10] craturs, but, sirs, it vexes me sair
Tae mind on the lee they tauld him tae fetch him:
    still
I see him steppin oot o thon sedan chair.
¹¹playful Wi the daffin[11] licht in his een,
Thinkin' tae crack wi' a freen:
He wisna sae debonair
At the hinner-end, when we had him bound. Yon
    ill
Judas-lee wrings me still.

Aye, mebbe he's juist as weel in yon warld o his ain
Whaur he sings o young love i' the springtime.
    Hearken the noo.
As blithe as a laverock's liltin, the bonny strain,
Ca'd *The Birks o Invermay*, an' a bonny voice too.
'Sir Precentor', they ca'd the loon,
I' the taverns o Embro toun,
Aye warblin, warblin away
Till ye fancy ye smell the flourish on the spray
Owre the daft heid, crouned wi the strae.

Atweel, it'll no be lang noo; he hoasts[12] that sair,   [12]coughs
I jalouse[13] he will sune win free o yon waesome den,   [13]surmise
'Even as a bird out of the fowler's snare,'
As the Psalmist sings: an' better wi God than men.
'A poet, but brunt his rhymes.'
Dae ye tell me so? There are times when I ken that
      yon voice sae clear
Will ring even-on i' my ear,
Till the close o my mortal times.

Alice V. Stuart

Embro to the Ploy

In simmer, whan aa sorts foregether
in Embro to the ploy,[1]   [1]festival
folk seek out friens to hae a blether,[2]   [2]gossip
or faes they'd fain annoy;
smorit[3] wi' British Railways' reek   [3]smothered
frae Glesca or Glen Roy
or Wick, they come to hae a week
of cultivatit joy
                    or three,
in Embro to the ploy.

Americans wi routh[4] of dollars,   [4]plenty
wha drink our whisky neat,
wi Sasunachs and Oxford Scholars,
are eydent[5] for the treat   [5]eager
of music sedulously high-tie
at thirty-bob a seat;
Wop opera performed in Eyetie
to them's richt up their street,
                    they say,
in Embro to the ploy.

Furthgangan⁶ Embro folk come hame,
for three weeks in the year,
and find Auld Reekie no the same,

fu sturrit in a steir.⁷
The stane-faced biggins whaur they froze

and suppit puirshous⁸ leir
of cultural cauld-kale and brose

see cantraips⁹ unco queer
                                        thae days
in Embro to the ploy.

The auld High Schule, whaur monie a skelp
of triple-tonguit tawse
has gien a hyst-up and a help
towards Doctorates of Laws,
nou hears, for Ramsay's cantie rhyme,

loud pawmies¹⁰ of applause
frae folk that pey a pund a time
to sit on wudden raws
                                        gey hard
in Embro to the ploy.

The haly kirk's Assembly-haa
nou fairly coups the creel
wi Lindsay's Three Estaitis, braw
devices of the deil.
About our heids the satire stots
like hailstones till we reel;

the bawrs¹¹ are in auld-farrant¹² Scots,
it's maybe just as weill,
                                        imphm,
in Embro to the ploy.

The Northern British Embro Whigs
that stayed in Charlotte Square,

they fairly wad hae tined¹³ their wigs,
to see the Stuarts there,

the bleeding Earl of Moray and aa
weill-pentit and gey bare;
Our Queen and Princess, buskit braw,
enjoyed the hale affair
                    (See Press)
in Embro to the ploy.

Whan day's anomalies are cled
in decent shades of nicht,
the Castle is transmogrified
by braw electric licht.
The toure that bields[14] the Bruce's croun   [14]shelters
presents an unco sicht
mair sib to Wardour Street nor Scone,
                    says I
in Embro to the ploy.

The Café Royal and Abbotsford
are filled wi orra[15] folk   [15]strangers
whaes stock-in-trade's the scrievit[16] word,   [16]written
or twicet-scrievit joke.
Brains, weak or strang, in heavy beer,
or ordinary, soak.
Quo yin: This yill is aafie dear,
I hae nae clinks[17] in poke,   [17]change
                    nor fauldan-money,
in Embro to the ploy.

The Auld Assembly-Rooms, whaur Scott
foregethert wi his fiers,[18]   [18]comrades
nou see a gey kenspeckle[19] lot   [19]con-
ablow the chandeliers.   spicuous
Til Embro drouths the Festival Club
a richt godsend appears;
it's something new to find a pub
that gaes on serving beers
                    eftir hours
in Embro to the ploy.

They toddle hame doun lit-up streets
filled wi synthetic joy;
aweill, the year brings few sic treats
and muckle to annoy.
There's monie hartsom[20] braw high-jinks
mixed up in this alloy
in simmer, whan aa sorts foregather
in Embro to the ploy.

[20]encouraging

Robert Garioch

The Coming of the Wee Malkies

[1]drop
[2]off

Whit'll ye dae when the wee Malkies come,
if they dreep[1] doon affy[2] the wash-hoose dyke

[3]put out of order

an pit the hems oan[3] the sterrheid light,
an play wee-heidies oan the clean close-wa',

[4]burst

an blooter[4] yir windae in wi' the ba',
missis, whit'll ye dae?

[5]knock
[6]milk-sop children
[7]turn somersaults
[8]empty

Whit'll ye dae when the wee Malkies come,
if they chap yir door an' choke yir drains,
an caw[5] the feet fae yir sapsy weans,[6]
an tummle thur wulkies[7] through yir sheets,
an tim[8] thur ashes oot in the street,
missis, whit'll ye dae?

[9]toilet
[10]butt with the head
[11]shuffling
[12]phrase used to call a halt in a game for a breach of the rules

Whit'll ye dae when the wee Malkies come,
if they chuck thur screwtaps doon the pan,[9]
an stick the heid oan[10] the sanit'ry man;
when ye hear thum come shauchlin[11] doon yir loaby,
chantin', 'Wee Malkies! The gemme's . . . a bogey!'[12]
Haw, missis, whit'll ye dae?

Stephen Mulrine

The Gowk[1]

Half doun the hill, whaur fa's the linn[2]
Far frae the flaught[3] o' fowk,
I saw upon a lanely whin
A lanely singin' gowk:
Cuckoo, cuckoo;
And at my back
The howie[4] hill stüde up and spak:
Cuckoo, cuckoo.

There was nae soun': the loupin'[5] linn
Hung frostit in its fa':
Nae bird was on the lanely whin
Sae white wi' fleurs o' snaw:
Cuckoo, cuckoo;
I stude stane still
And saftly spak the howie hill:
Cuckoo, cuckoo.

William Soutar

The Eemis Stane

I' the how-dumb-deid[1] o' the cauld hairst[2] nicht
The warl'[3] like an eemis[4] stane
Wags i' the lift;[5]
An' my eerie memories fa'
Like a yowdendrift.[6]

Like a yowdendrift so's I couldna read
The words cut oot i' the stane
Had the fug[7] o' fame
An' history's hazelraw[8]
No' yirdit[9] thaim.

Hugh MacDiarmid

Jamie the Saxt

'*Jamie the Saxt*', by Robert McLellan, is a historical play, in four acts, about the troubles of James VI of Scotland before he became James I of England. The play is in Scots. It tells of the troubles of the King with his ambitious and treacherous nobles: it also tells of his handsome queen, his belief in witchcraft, and of his 'keeping-in' with the English Ambassador. This was so that Queen Elizabeth would look kindly upon his claim to the throne of England.

ACT IV sees the eccentric but clever king triumphant over his nobles (for the time being) and getting the better of the English Ambassador.

ACT IV

'Nicoll Eduardis hous in Nithreis Wynd'
Edinburgh, XV September, 1594.   *Late afternoon*

The shutters are wide open, giving a view of the opposite side of the Wynd in the light of a sunny afternoon in Autumn.

MISTRESS EDWARD *is sitting on a bench at the window, working on a piece of tapestry attached to a frame.* RAB *appears at the door behind her.*

MRS E:	Nou Rab, ye needna ask me that. Ye'll hae to hear what yer maister says.

(Nicoll *enters as she speaks*)

NICOLL:	What's this?
MRS E:	He wants oot in time to see a hangin.
RAB:	The twa men o Bothwell's that struck siller oot o a souther.[1] They're to be hurlt through the Toun.
NICOLL:	We'll see. We'll see. Were ye oot at the hairst?
RAB:	Ay.
NICOLL:	And hoo's it gaun?

[1] stole from a man from the South

128

RAB:	They were scythin the last rig whan I cam awa.
NICOLL:	Is aa that's cut stookit?
RAB:	Ay.
NICOLL:	Grand. The wather can dae what it likes nou. Weill, lad, ye can tak yer supper in yer pooch and gang to the hangin whan the booth's lockit. And let it be a lesson to ye neir to wrang yer maister, be he King, Lord, or Toun Merchant. Awa wi' ye.

(Rab *leaves*)

MRS E:	Sae Bothwell's up to his tricks again?
NICOLL:	Ay, but he's gaen ower faur this time. He'll hae nae sympathy nou. Gin ilka body wi' a toom pooch[2] were to stert makin his ain siller there wad be nae profit in tred[3] at aa.

(Rab *enters suddenly*)

RAB:	Guess wha's here!
MRS E:	Wha?
RAB:	Her Grace, wi the Laird Logie and the Danish leddy!
MRS E:	Oh dear me, and I'm sic a sicht! O Nicoll! Oh what'll I dae?
NICOLL:	Tach, wamman, ye're aa richt. Fetch them up, Rab.

(Rab *leaves hurriedly, and* Nicoll *goes to the door*)

NICOLL:	(*At the door*) Weill, weill, weill. (*The* Queen *appears, with* Logie *and* Margaret Vinstar *behind her*) Come awa in, yer Grace. Sae ye're back frae Stirlin?

(*The three enter. Appropriate bows, bobs and curtsies*)

[2]empty pocket
[3]trade

MRS E:	Yer Grace, this *is* a surprise!
THE QUEEN:	We thocht we wad caa in for a meenit in the passin. We canna bide lang. We shanna sit. But ye are pleased to see us, eh?
MRS E:	Yer Grace, ye hae dune us an honour.
NICOLL:	Ye hae that.
MRS E:	And my Leddy Vinstar.
NICOLL:	Ay, Laird, sae ye brak oot ae jeyl[4] and landit yersell in anither.
MRS E:	What things men say! Dinna heed him, Leddy Margaret. But I thocht, weill, ye se—
THE QUEEN:	Ye woner to see them back at Coort, eh?
MRS E:	Ay weill, I thocht the Laird wad still be in his Grace's black books.
THE QUEEN:	Na na. I missed my Margaret and wantit her back, sae I twistit him roun my finger. Logie is paurdont.
MRS E:	I'm gled to hear it.
THE QUEEN:	His Grace gat redd o Bothwell and wantit the Chancellor back at the Coort. I said no. I said that gin he didna allou Margaret back wi her Logie he wad hae nae Chancellor. And what could he say?
MRS E:	And the Chancellor's back? Times hae cheynged, eh?
THE QUEEN:	Mistress Edward, it is different aa thegither. There is haurdly an auld face left. Atholl is put to the horn,[5] Ochiltree is oot wi Bothwell, and Spynie is in jeyle, puir man. Logie has been gey luckie.
NICOLL:	He has that.
THE QUEEN:	Weill, ye see, he mairrit my Margaret, and the rest didna. But the Chancellor, Mistress Edward, ye suld see. He is a cheynged man. He licks my shune like a dug. And he taks pains.
MRS E:	Pains?

[4]one prison
[5]proclaimed a rebel

THE QUEEN:	Ay, and they are gey sair. He will talk and talk and then, aa at ance, he will twist his face and girn and haud his back. Puir man, I feel sorry, but it gars me lauch.
NICOLL:	I suld think sae.
MRS E:	But ye haena said onything yet aboot the big event in yer ain life.
THE QUEEN:	(*Coyly*) Ah, Mistress Edward, haud yer tongue.
MRS E:	Is the young Prince keepin weill. What is he like?
THE QUEEN:	Ah weill (*shrugging humorously*) he is like his faither.
MRS E:	(*Forgetting herself*) Aw. (*Recovering*). I hear the young Prince gat some gey grand praisents.
THE QUEEN:	(*Brightening*) Oh Mistress Edward, it wad hae taen awa yer braith. Frae the States o' Holland there was a gowden box, and inside, written in gowden letters, a promise to pey the young Prince a yearly pension o a thoosand guilders.
MRS E:	A thoosand guilders! Dear me.
THE QUEEN:	It is a lot. And gowden cups! Oh Mistress Edward, the wecht! Sir James Melville stude aside me to tak the heavy things, and he could hardly haud them. And there were precious stanes frae my ain country, and mair gowden cups, and a fancy kist,[6] staunin on legs, frae her Majesty o England.
MRS E:	Mercy me, he's a luckie bairn. And he has a gey hantle[7] o titles for ane no oot o his creddle.
THE QUEEN:	Titles! What a rigmarole! I hae it aff by hairt. 'The richt excellent, high and magnanimous Frederick Henry Henry Frederick' —he is caa'd efter my faither ye see, and the faither o her Majesty doun bye, and we hae

[6]chest
[7]a large number

	it baith weys to please everybody—but I am wanert aff—'Frederick Henry Henry Frederick by the Grace o God Baron o Renfrew, Lord o the Isles, Earl o Carrick, Duke o Rothesay, Prince and Great Steward o Scotland.'
MRS E:	It's a gey lang screed that.
THE QUEEN:	It is ower muckle. I caa him 'Wee Henry'.
MRS E:	(*Laughing*) Ay, it'll be a lot mair convenient. But I thocht ye wad hae caa'd him by yer ain faither's name.
THE QUEEN:	Na na, we caa him by the English name, for some day he will be English King. But Mistress Edward, we canna bide.[8] We hae to see the Provost. Ye maun come to the Palace, some day sune and see Wee Henry for yersell.
MRS E:	Yer Grace, I'll tak ye at yer word.
THE QUEEN:	Dae. We sall be pleased to see ye. (*Bobbing*) Bailie, I bid ye guid efternune.
NICOLL:	(*Bowing*) Guid efternune, yer Grace. I'm sorry ye canna bide. And I'm sorry his Grace isna wi ye.
THE QUEEN:	Huh! *He* is doun the Coogait, at the printers'.
NICOLL:	Aye at books yet.
THE QUEEN:	Aye at books. (*Bobbing*) Mistress Edward, fare ye weill. (*Exit*)
MRS E:	(*With a curtsy*) Fare ye weill, yer Grace. (*Bobbing*) And ye, my Leddy. (*Bobbing*) And ye tae, Laird. See and bide oot o jeyl this time.
NICOLL:	My Leddy Margaret'll see to that.
LOGIE:	(*Bowing*) My wild days are bye nou, Mistress Edward. Guid efternune, Bailie.
NICOLL:	I'll come doun.

> (*He follows the visitors out. Mistress Edward watches them go, takes a seat by the window, sits*

[8]stay

and wipes her eyes as a few tears gather. Nicoll
enters)

NICOLL: What's wrang wi ye?
MRS E: I was haein a wee bit greit.
NICOLL: What aboot?
MRS E: I was juist thinkin.
NICOLL: What?
MRS E: Weill, her Grace is sae cantie[9] the nou. I was
            thinkin what a peety it is that the Lord God
            haesna seen fit to gie us the blessin o a
            bairn tae.
NICOLL: Hoot, wumman, think o yer age.
MRS E: Ay, but still.
NICOLL: Tach!

            (Rab *enters*)

RAB: Here's Bailie Morison!
NICOLL: Eh! What daes he want?
RAB: He wants to see ye.
NICOLL: Nae dout. Fetch him up. (Rab *leaves*) He can
            keep his neb oot o naething. He'll hae heard
            that I hae Maister Bruce comin up.
MRS E: I hope he saw her Grace leavin. It'll gie him
            something to tell his wife.
BAILIE M: (*Outside*) Are ye there, Nicoll?
NICOLL: Ay, Bailie, come in.

            (Bailie Morison *enters, with* Rab *behind
            him*)

MRS E: Guid efternune, Bailie.
BAILIE M: Guid efternune, Mistress Edward.
RAB: Can I gang nou?
NICOLL: Hae ye lockit the booth?
RAB: Ay.
NICOLL: Awa then. (Rab *shoots off.* Mistress Edward
            goes to the awmrie[10] *for a bottle and glasses*) Sit
            doun, Bailie.

[9]cheerful
[10]cupboard

133

MRS E:	Ye'll hae a dram?
BAILIE M:	Weill ay, I will, thank ye. It's gey drouthy[11] wather. I saw her Grace leavin the nou.
MRS E:	(*Pouring drinks*) Oh ay, she aye taks a rin up if she's anywhaur near.
BAILIE M:	Ay, ye seem to be gey weill ben. (*Accepting drink*) Thank ye. Yer guid health.
NICOLL:	(*Also served*) Guid health.
MRS E:	Thank ye.

(*She bobs and leaves by the dining-room door*)

BAILIE M:	I hear ye hae Maister Bruce comin up?
NICOLL:	Ay.
BAILIE M:	It'll be aboot siller for the raid against the Papists?
NICOLL:	Ay weill, I canna say ye're wrang.
BAILIE M	And hoo dae ye staun?
NICOLL:	Weill Bailie, I dout I can dae nae mair. His Grace is ower deep in my debt as it is.
BAILIE M:	That's my poseetion tae, in a wey.
NICOLL:	In a wey, eh?
BAILIE M:	Weill, ye see, I could afford to lend him mair gin he could offer guid security.
NICOLL:	Sae could I. But whaur will he fin that?
BAILIE M:	Think. Hae ye no heard aboot the christenin praisents that were brocht to the young Prince?
NICOLL:	Damn it, Bailie, we canna tak the bairn's christenin praisents!
BAILIE M:	I see nae hairm in it.
NICOLL:	It isna richt.
BAILIE M:	Man, it's oor ae chance o gettin a bawbee o oor siller back. There's eneugh gowd, frae what I hear, to cover baith what he owes us the nou and a new advance as weill. In fact, Nicoll, it wad be a grand stroke o business.
NICOLL:	He wadna hear o't.
BAILIE M:	Weill—.

[11]thirsty

134

NICOLL:	Na na.

(Mistress Edward *comes to the door*)

MRS E:	Nicoll, here's Maister Bruce.
NICOLL:	Haud on, then. He's aye rantin against self-indulgence. Gie me yer gless, Bailie. Fetch him nou.

(*He hurriedly hides the bottle and glasses as* Mistress Edward *goes for* Bruce)

NICOLL:	(*As* Bruce *appears*) Come in, Maister Bruce. *Come in.* (Mistress Edward *retires and closes the door*) I hae Bailie Morison here.
BAILIE M:	(*Half rising*) Nicoll, if ye hae business to discuss I had mebbe better leave ye.
BRUCE:	My business micht concern ye tae, Bailie, sae dinna leave on my accoont.
NICOLL:	Maister Bruce, will ye sit doun?
BRUCE:	(*Sitting*) Thank ye.
NICOLL:	It's been grand wather for the hairst.
BAILIE M:	Deed ay. I haena seen the Muir wi sic bonnie raws o stooks on't for mony a lang year.
BRUCE:	The Lord has filled yer girnels, Bailie, as a sign and a portent. He wad hae ye return His liberality in the service o His cause.
BAILIE M:	Ay?
BRUCE:	Oor temporal ruler, as ye weill ken, is pledged to haud a raid against the Papist Lords, but he says he hasna the siller to pey for the men. That may be the truith, my freinds, and it may no, but gin the siller were brocht forrit he wad hae to stert.
NICOLL:	Ay, Maister Bruce, and what dae ye propose?
BRUCE:	I had thocht, Bailie, that an advance micht be made to the Croun at ance.
NICOLL:	Na.
BAILIE M:	Na.
BRUCE:	Think weill, my friends, afore ye harden yer

	hairts. The cause I ask ye to serve is the cause o the Kirk, and gin ye dinna serve it weill ye canna prosper. For hasna the Lord said ...
NICOLL:	Ay ay, Maister Bruce, but we arena in the Kirk the nou. This is a maitter o business. Ye ask us to mak an advance to the Croun, but the Croun's gey deep in oor debt as it is. It canna be dune, Maister Bruce.
BAILIE M:	Weill, Nicoll, I wadna say that. There micht be some ither wey.
NICOLL:	There's nae ither wey, I tell ye. The poseetion's hopeless frae the stert. If his Grace had his hairt in the raid it wad be a different maitter, but ye ken hou he led the last ane. Whan eir he gat near the Papists he pitched his camp till they had time to retreat, and the Hielands are braid enough to let that sort o ploy[12] gang on for years. The haill truith o the maitter is, Maister Bruce, that he winna lead the raid wi ony hairt till he has houndit doun Bothwell, and that ye winna let him dae.
BRUCE:	He can dae that whan he has first served God and the Kirk! Bothwell's soond in his releegion!

(*There is a faint commotion from far beyond the window*)

NICOLL:	He has nae scruples whaur siller's concerned. Listen to that! Twa o his men are bein hurlt through the Toun for makin coonterfeit thirty shillin pieces!
BRUCE:	It's anither o the Chancellor's fause chairges! Bothwell has naething to dae wi the men!
BAILIE M:	What's that!

(*Rab can be heard on the staircase shouting* 'Bailie Edward! Maister!')

[12]scheme

NICOLL: It's Rab!

(Rab *enters breathlessly*)

RAB: There's a fecht on at the Nether Bow Port!
Johnstones and Maxwells! The Johnstones
raidit the Nether Tolbooth to let their twa
freends oot, and the Maxwells that brocht
them in cam doun the Hie Gait to stop it!
The Toun Gaird's trying to clear the causey!

NICOLL: Guid God! Help me on wi my gear, Rab!

(Nicoll *and* Rab *hurry out through the
dining-room door. Bailie Morison goes to the
window*)

BAILIE M: Here's his Grace, fleein for his life, wi the
Chancellor pechin[13] ahint him! (Bruce *goes
over beside him*) I believe he's coming here!

(Mistress Edward *enters from the dining-
room*)

MRS E: What's aa the steer? I'm shair Nicoll
daesna hae to gang fechtin! He'll be
slauchtert! It isna richt!

(The King *is heard on the staircase shouting
'Nicoll Edward! Nicoll, ye deil!'*)

BAILIE M: It's his Grace.

(The King *enters in disarray*)

THE KING: Mistress Edward, gie me a dram! I hae been
gey near shot doun, hackit to bits, and
staned to daith!

(Mistress Edward *hastens to pour him a
drink. Nicoll appears at the dining-room door,
strapping on his gear*)

NICOLL: What's wrang, yer Grace?
THE KING: What's wrang! Yer Toun isna safe! That's

[13]breathing heavily

	what's wrang! It's fou o Border reivers fleein at ilk[14] ither's throats!
RAB:	(*Coming in behind* Nicoll *with his pistols*) It's the Johnstones, yer Grace! They were trying to brek doun the doors o the Nether Tolbooth and let oot Bothwell's twa men!
THE KING:	Bothwell! I micht hae kent it! There'll be nae peace in the country till the blaggard's ablow the grun! (*Accepting a glass from* Mistress Edward) Thank ye Mistress Edward. (*The* Chancellor *appears at the door, breathing heavily*) Ay, Jock, come in and sit doun. Gie him a dram tae, guid wumman, for he's worn oot.

(Maitland *slumps into a chair, and* Mistress Edward *goes to fetch him a drink. The Town bell begins to ring*)

NICOLL:	(*Completing his preparations*) There's the Town bell, thank God. It'll bring the men up frae the hairst. Hurry oot, Rab. Bailie Morison, dinna staun there gawpin. Come on hame for yer gear.[15]
MRS E:	Oh Nicoll, watch yersell.
NICOLL:	(*Leaving quickly*) Ay ay.

(Rab *and* Bailie Morison *follow him out*)

MRS E:	(*Dabbing her eyes*) Oh I hope he'll be aa richt.
THE KING:	Ay ay, Mistress, he'll be aa richt. He's as strang as a bull. Are ye comin roun, Jock?
MAITLAND:	(*Busy with his glass*) Gie me time.
MRS E:	(*Suddenly remembering*) Her Grace was here no lang syne. I wonder if she'll be aa richt.
THE KING:	Her Grace, eh? Whaur did she gang?
MRS E:	She left to gang to the Provost's.
THE KING:	There's nae need to worry then. The fechtin's aa ablow the Tron.
MRS E:	I think I'll gang up to the mooth o the Wynd and hae a look, though. It micht be better.

[14]each
[15]sword, armour, etc.

138

| THE KING: | Watch yersell, then. |
| MRS E: | Ay ay. |

(She goes out in a state of agitation)

THE KING:	Weill, Maister Bruce, what are ye staunin glowering at? Can the like o ye dae naething? Or are ye sae thick wi Bothwell that ye want his freends to win?
BRUCE:	Ye hae nae richt to blame Bothwell! He was first put to the horn on a fause chairge, and whan he was adjudged guiltless, he gat nae remission! And that in spite o yer promise, written by yer ain haund!
THE KING:	My promise was cancelled by the Three Estates! And he has little to complain o, the Lord kens.
BRUCE:	He left the country! He gaed to England!
THE KING:	To lie low and plot anither raid! Ye talk aboot brekin promises, Maister Bruce, but if Bothwell has his match in the haill o Christendom he'll be gey ill to fin!
BRUCE:	His match is praisent in this very room!
THE KING:	Jock! Did ye hear that?
MAITLAND:	Gin I werena auld and dune I wad split his croun!
BRUCE:	I spak the truith, Maitland, as weill ye ken! Didna the King promise that ye and Hume suld be keepit frae the Coort?
THE KING:	Guid God, ye canna object to Jock here! He's a dune auld man.
BRUCE:	And Hume? Is he dune?
THE KING:	Ye ken he's convertit! I argued him roun mysell. He's as guid a Protestant as there is in the country.
BRUCE:	He's like a' the ithers ye hae aboot ye, a hypocrite that wad raither ye spent the revenues o the Croun on his ain profligate pleasures nor in the service o God's Kirk! But I tell ye, Jamie Stewart, King though ye be, that gin ye dinna rouse yersell to dae

	the wark that the Lord has committitt to yer haund, the Kirk sall rise in its strength and act withoot ye!
THE KING:	Huh! They'd look a bonnie lot! Eh, Jock can ye see them? (Maitland *snorts*) Weill I ken what they'd be like, Maister Bruce: a rabble o puir gowks airmed wi heuks.[16] And nae dout yersell and Andrew Melville wad lead them?
BRUCE:	They wad be led by my Lord Bothwell!
THE KING:	Oho, ye deil!
MAITLAND:	(*Pushing back his chair and gripping his hilt*) Watch what ye say, sir! Yer words micht cost ye dear!
BRUCE:	Ye daurna touch me, and ye ken it! The folk o the Toun wad stane ye!
MAITLAND:	(*Stepping forward and drawing*) I wad tak the risk!
BRUCE:	Tak it, and may the Lord accurse ye! May aa the maledictions that fell upon Judas, Pilate, Herod and the Jews, aa the troubles that fell upon the city o Jerusalem, aa the plagues—
	(*He breaks off, as* Maitland *seems suddenly to be seized with pain. The Town bell stops ringing*)
MAITLAND:	(*Writhing back into his chair and dropping his sword*) Oh. Oh. Oh.
	(*The* King *and* Bruce *stare at him in amazement.* Mistress Edward *enters hurriedly from the staircase*)
MRS E:	Yer Grace! (*Noticing* Maitland) Guidness gracious, what's wrang?
THE KING:	That deil's been cursin Jock. It's brocht on his pains.
MRS E:	(*Reproachfully*) Oh, Maister Bruce.

[16]short scythes

140

THE KING: I'll hae him tried for witchcraft! Sit up, Jock, and tak anither moothfou. That's richt. Are ye feelin better?

MAITLAND: Gie me time.

MRS E: Yer Grace, my Lord Lennox and Nicoll are bringing a man doun the Wynd.

THE KING: A man, eh?

MRS E: Ay, by the scruff o the neck. Here they are nou.

(They look to the door. Lennox enters)

LENNOX: *(To Nicoll outside)* Bring him in, Nicoll. *(Nicoll enters leading a stranger by the shoulder. Lennox steps forward and hands the King a letter)* Yer Grace, hae a look at that.

THE KING: *(Indicating the stranger)* Wha's this?

LENNOX: It's Sir Robert Bowes' new English servant.

THE KING: And what's this? Whaur did ye fin it?

LENNOX: I was in the Hie Gait whan the steer[17] stertit. Juist whan it was at its heicht a man made to ride up the Toun frae the Black Friar's Wynd and was dung aff his horse by a stray shot. This man ran forrit and rypit[18] his pooches. It was that he was efter, for whan eir he fand it he made to rin awa.

THE KING: *(Unrolling it)* Oho! No a word on it! Conspeeracy! Weill weill, we hae dealt wi blanks afore. Mistress Edward, rin ben to the kitchen and fetch a bit o flannel and a hot airn. Hurry! We'll sune see what's at the bottom o this. *(Mistress Edward hurries out by the dining-room door. To the stranger)* Ay ay, my man, sae ye hae been foun wi' a secret document in yer possession? Pou him forrit Nicoll, and put yer sword to his hin end. *(Nicoll obeys)* Was this letter for Sir Robert Bowes? *(Silence)* Was it, I'm askin? Nicol, gar him speak.

[17]uproar
[18]rummaged through

141

NICOLL:	(*Jabbing the stranger*) Answer whan ye're telt!
STRANGER:	(*Turning on him indignantly, and speaking with a Cockney accent*) Avaunt, thou pock-faced villain, sheathe thy sword! I know not what thy master asketh!
THE KING:	What is he sayin? Tak him by the collar!

(Nicoll *obeys*)

STRANGER:	Unhand me or I'll kick thy paunch, thou bottled-nosed bully!
THE KING:	Jab him again, Nicoll!

(Nicoll *obeys*)

STRANGER:	Oh!
NICOLL:	Staun at peace, see!
STRANGER:	Peace! God's light, if this be peace! Call for my master!
THE KING:	He said something about his maister! I'll try him in English. Listen, my man. Art thou the servant of Sir Robert Bowes?
STRANGER:	He is my master! Call him here!
THE KING:	Ay ay, but listen. Did Sir Robert Bowes send thee to obtain this letter?
STRANGER:	Thy scurvy dog of a servant choketh me!
THE KING:	Eh? What is he sayin, Jock?
MAITLAND:	It bates me.
THE KING:	Listen again. Did Sir Robert Bowes send thee to obtain this letter?
STRANGER:	He is my master!
MAITLAND:	Maister! It's aa he can think o!
THE KING:	He's donnart![19] Letter, my man! Letter! Dae ye no ken what letter means? Dost thou see this letter?
STRANGER:	How can I see? He has me by the throat! Order thy varlet off!
THE KING:	It's hopeless. I wish Sir Jamie Melville was here. He kens aa their tongues.
LENNOX:	He's at Halhill the nou.

[19]dazed, stupid

THE KING:	He's aye awa whan he's maist needit. But we'll persevere. We'll tak him word by word. Dae ye hear? Dost thou hear? We shall speak each word separately. Dost thou understand letter?
STRANGER:	Call for my master! He will tell thee all!
MAITLAND:	Maister again!
THE KING:	We're at letter the nou, no maister! I'm haudin it up! Look at it!
STRANGER:	I know not what thou sayest!
THE KING:	What was that?
MAITLAND:	I didna catch it.
THE KING:	Can ye no speak ae word at a time?
MAITLAND:	Say it in English.
THE KING:	Ay ay, I forgot. Canst thou not speak each word separately?
STRANGER:	God grant me patience! Dost thou not follow Master? Master, thou addle-pate! Master!
THE KING:	Guid God!
MAITLAND:	He's at it yet!
THE KING:	I dinna like his mainner, aither.
MAITLAND:	Naither dae I. Put him in the jougs.[20]
THE KING:	Dae ye ken what the jougs are? Dae ye ken what the rack is? Dost thou understand gallows?
STRANGER:	Call for my master!
THE KING:	Guid God Almichty! Tak him oot and droun him!
MAITLAND:	Put him in the jougs!
THE KING:	And fetch his maister! We'll see what he has to say! Dinna say what we're efter, though. We'll tak him by surprise.
NICOLL:	Aa richt, yer Grace. (*Dragging the* stranger *out*) Come on, see.
STRANGER:	Call for my master! Call for my master! (*Turning his attention from the* King *to* Nicoll) Oh thou lousy, damned, abominable rogue!

[20] a hinged iron collar attached to a post or wall and locked round the neck of the offender

NICOLL :   Haud yer tongue or I'll clowt[21] ye!

(*He bundles the* stranger *out by the staircase door.* Mistress Edward *enters from the dining-room with a piece of flannel and a hot iron*)

MRS E :   Here ye are, yer Grace. I was as quick as I could manage.

THE KING :   Ye haena been lang. Gie me the flannel. We'll spread it here. Then the letter, flat oot. Haud it doun, Jock, till I fold the flannel ower it. Nou put down the airn. (Mistress Edward *lays the iron on the table. The King picks it up*) Hou hot is it? (*He tests it*) Ph! Grand. It's juist richt. Nou watch this.

(*He starts to iron carefully over the letter*)

MRS E :   Whaur's Nicoll, yer Grace?

THE KING :   He's awa to the Tolbooth wi the English-man. Wheesht the nou. We'll sune see what Sir Robert's up to. (*He puts down the iron and lifts the flannel*) Look, Jock, it's up!

MAITLAND :   It is that!

THE KING :   It's in Sir Robert's haund! Juist what I thocht! Sir Robert's servant maun hae gien it to the horseman in the first place! Nou let me see. (*He reads excitedly*) It's fou o ciphers! Jock, ye ken the English code! Wha's Argomartes? Bothwell, eh?

MAITLAND :   Nane else! Is it for him?

THE KING :   It is! By God, I hae Sir Robert nou! (*He reads*) America! That's the English Queen hersell!

MAITLAND :   America, ay!

THE KING :   Oho, then listen to this! 'Thou (That's Bothwell) didst by thine own unreasonable demeanour render thyself too weak to serve America further, and cannot complain that America now leaves thee to furnish thine own purse.' Oho, eh! It's what I aye said!

[21]a smack, usually about the head

144

He's been in her pey aa alang! (*He reads*)
But there's a bit here I canna richt mak oot.
'As for thy latest threat, America hath
strong hopes that through vee ane emm
thirty-sax pund sterlin . . .'

MAITLAND: The Preachers!

THE KING: Eh! By God, Maister Bruce, sae ye're in
towe wi Sir Robert tae!

BRUCE: It's a lee! There's a mistake!

THE KING: Haud yer tongue and we'll see. It says here
'America hath strong hopes that through the
Preachers she may force Petrea . . .' That's
me! What rank black ineequity!

MAITLAND: Force ye to what!

THE KING: 'To rise against Chanus'.

MAITLAND: Huntly!

THE KING: Juist that! Listen! 'to rise against Chanus in
such strength that thy support will avail
him nothing.' Guid God! Thy support!
Bothwell's!

MAITLAND: Support for Huntly!

THE KING: It canna be!

(*They peer excitedly into the letter. There is a
commotion below the window*)

MRS E: There's a steer on the stairs!

(Rab *comes to the door*)
(*He stands back.* Morton *enters*)

MORTON: Yer Grace, I hae Colville here! He's gien
himsell up!

THE KING: What! Whaur is he?

MORTON: I hae him here! He says he wants to speak
to ye at ance!

THE KING: Dinna let him near me! It's a plot!

MORTON: He says he has news for ye alane!

THE KING: It's a trick, I tell ye! Is he airmed?

MORTON: Na.

THE KING: Lodovick! Staun bye and draw! Jock!

Whaur's yer sword? Pick it up! See that he daesna win near me!

MORTON: Sall I fetch him?

THE KING: Ye're shair he has nae weapons?

MORTON: Ay.

THE KING: Then let him come.

(*They stand expectant.* Morton *leaves. In a moment he returns and stands within the door.* Colville *enters stained with travel, and throws himself at the* King's *feet. The* King *shrinks back*)

THE KING: Keep back!

COLVILLE: Maist Clement Prince.

THE KING: Ye hae said that afore! What dae ye want?

COLVILLE: (*Grovelling*) Yer Grace, I hae focht against ye in bygaen times, but I actit as my conscience dictatit.

THE KING: Ye leear, ye did it for Bothwell and his English siller!

COLVILLE: The Lord kens, yer Grace, that I thocht he was soond in doctrine. I renounce him nou!

THE KING: Eh?

COLVILLE: He's jeynt the Papist Lords for Spanish gowd!

THE KING: (*Quietly*) Say that again.

COLVILLE: He's at Kirk o Memure wi Huntly and the ithers! They hae pledged themsells to kidnap the young Prince and murder Hume and Maitland.

THE KING: (*As* Maitland *gasps*) The fiend o hell! Wha telt ye that?

COLVILLE: I hae kent it aa alang! I wantit to mak shair! Yer Grace, ye'll paurdon me? I'll serve ye weill!

THE KING: I wad paurdon the Deil himsell for that news! It's like a dream come true! My warst enemy destroyed by his ain folly! Aa my troubles washt awa by ae turn o the tide!

	It's lauchable. It's rideeculous. It's a slap in the face to the Kirk and England baith. Ay, Maister Bruce, ye may weill look dumfounert! That's yer Bothwell for ye! That's the man that was to lead the godly in the service o the Lord! But dinna tak it ill, man! The Lord sall be served! I'll hound doun the Papists for ye nou! (*With a quick change of manner*) Man, Jock, look at him. He daesna seem pleased.
MAITLAND:	It's ower big a dose for ae gulp.
THE KING:	That'll teach ye, my man, that it's in the Croun and no in the Assemblies o yer Kirk that the Lord invests His authority, for has he no by this very move entrustit leadership to me, and gart ye lick yer vomit!
BRUCE:	His will's beyond yer comprehension!
THE KING:	His will's as clear as the licht o day! He has peyntit me oot as His airthly Lieutenant! Awa to yer colleagues, man, and tell them the news! Tell them their idol has turnt idolator! Let them cry frae ilka pulpit that the hour has come at last, whan the King sall lead the godly in the service o the Lord, and Bothwell and the Papists sall perish thegither!
BRUCE:	May ye hae the Lord's help in the task, for ye'll fail withoot it!

(*He marches out*)

THE KING:	Hoho, he didna like it! He lost his tongue athegither! God, it's miraculous! Colville, I'll spare yer heid, man, for ye hae served me weill.
COLVILLE:	(*Kissing the* King's *hand*) Maist Clement Prince. Maist Noble King.
THE KING:	I haena paurdont ye yet, mind. Ye'll hae to tell me aa ye ken.
COLVILLE:	I hae copies o aa their documents, yer Grace.

THE KING:	They're yer ain wark, nae dout. Awa wi ye. (Colville *kisses his foot*) Man, ye're a scunner.[22] Watch him weill, my Lord. (Morton *bows*) Rise up aff the flair man, and tak yersell oot o my sicht! (Colville *bows himself elaborately out of the room. Morton bows and follows him*) He turns my stamack, but he'll be worth his wecht in gowd. Lodovick! Caa my Cooncil for eicht o'clock.
LENNOX:	Very weill, yer Grace.

(He bows and leaves)

THE KING:	(*Reaching for the bottle*) Weill, Jock, it's been a grand efternune. Eh, Mistress?
MRS E:	It has that, yer Grace. Sall I tak the airn?
THE KING:	Leave it. I want it. I'm expectin Sir Robert.
MRS E:	Very weill, yer Grace. I'll leave ye, I think, and hae the table laid. (*Knowingly*) Will ye bide for supper?
THE KING:	(*Joyfully*) Mistress Edward, ye're the best freend I hae! I'll clap my sword to yer guid man's back and say 'Arise Sir Nicoll'!
MRS E:	Na na, yer Grace, dinna dae that. The Kirk wad turn against him. Aa the tred in black claith wad gang to Tam MacDowell. Wait till he's retired.
THE KING:	Aa richt, what eir ye please. (*Eagerly*) What's in the pat?
MRS E:	Cock-a-leekie.
THE KING:	Ye maun hae kent I was comin!
MRS E:	(*Bobbing*) I ken ye like it.
THE KING:	I dae that. (Mistress Edward *leaves*) Jock, I'm bothert aboot siller. It'll tak a lot to cairry on a raid in the Hielands.
MAITLAND:	(*Who has been helping himself from the bottle*) Damn it, man, ye hae eneugh gowd at Stirlin to pey for a dizzen raids, if ye juist had the gumption[23] to use it.

[22]a man to make others sick
[23]commonsense

THE KING: Na na, Jock! Anna wadna hear o it! She
              wad flee oot at me! I wadna hae the life o a
              dug! Dinna stert that again!
MAITLAND: It's the ae wey oot.
THE KING: It canna be! We maun fin some ither! And
              it maun be sune. My haill hairt's set on
              stertin at ance. Man, think—
MAITLAND: Wheesht!
THE KING: Here they are! It's Sir Robert! By God, I'll
              gar him wriggle! Ye'll hae the time o yer
              life nou!

              (Nicoll *enters*)

NICOLL: Here's Sir Robert.

              (Sir Robert *enters*. Nicoll *withdraws*. The
              King *affects a heavy scowl*)

SIR ROBERT: (*Puzzled*) Your Majesty?
THE KING: Weill?
SIR ROBERT: You seem hostile.
THE KING: Daes it surprise ye?
SIR ROBERT: It doth, your Majesty, immediately.
THE KING: What dae ye think o that, Jock? He's fair
              astoundit!

              (Maitland *gives a little bark of laughter*)

SIR ROBERT: (*Indignantly*) My Lord! Your Majesty!
THE KING: Ay ay, Sir Robert, wark up yer indignation!
              But ye dinna ken what's comin! Dae ye see
              that airn? Dae ye see that bit o flannel? Dae
              ye see this letter? Ay, Sir Robert, ye may
              weill turn pale. Ye may weill gaup like a
              frichtent fish. Ye're a proved plotter, a
              briber o traitors, a hirer o murderers!
              Whan I think hoo ye hae leived amang us,
              respectit by gentle and simple in the Toun,
              treatit like a Lord at Coort, honoured wi'
              my ain freendship and invitit often to my
              very table, I tak a haill-hairtit scunner at
              human nature! There's nae kent form o

torture, nae wey o inflictin daith, that isna ower guid for ye! Ye're waur not the warst auld beldam witch that was eir brunt to cinders!

SIR ROBERT: Your Majesty, I am but an instrument of my country's policy.

THE KING: Policy! Jock, he said policy! (Maitland *snorts*) Sir Robert, yer mistress daesna ken what policy is. She wantit to stop the plottin o the Papists, and aa she could think wi was to mak Bothwell sic a terror to the country that I had to look to the Papists for help.

SIR ROBERT: I think she attributed your friendship with the Papists, your Majesty, to your hatred of the Protestant Church.

THE KING: The Protestant Kirk! It's a Presbyterian Kirk! They winna acknowledge their Sovereign as their speeritual heid! My fecht wi the Kirk, Sir Robert, is a fecht against government frae the pulpit, and yer mistress suld be the last to encourage that!

SIR ROBERT: Your Majesty, there was no question of such encouragement. My mistress feared Spanish invasion and the loss of her throne.

THE KING: Spanish invasion! Did she think for a meenit that I wad jeyn wi' Spain to put Phillip on the throne o England and destroy my ain claim to succeed her! Ye wad think Sir Robert, that I had nae intelligence at aa!

SIR ROBERT: Your Majesty, I assure you.

THE KING: Oh ay, Sir Robert, try to win me roun, but I tell ye that gin I had nae mair sense nor to waste guid siller on a treacherous blaggard like Bothwell I wad droun mysell in the nearest dub. Dae ye ken what he's dune? He's jeynt the Papists!

SIR ROBERT: (*Slightly startled*) I thought it possible.

THE KING: Ye thocht it possible!

SIR ROBERT: I did, your Majesty, as you will realize from my letter.

THE KING:	I realize frae yer letter that ye were gaun to try to force my haund through the Kirk. Dinna try to mak oot Sir Robert, that ye thocht I wad need ony forcin if Bothwell turnt his coat!
SIR ROBERT:	Am I to understand, your Majesty, that the Papist Lords will be attacked?
THE KING:	They will, by God, as sune as I can fin the siller!
SIR ROBERT:	(*Airily*) Then, your Majesty, all is well. I am certain that the Queen my mistress, when she hath heard of your resolve, will endow you with undreamt of wealth.
THE KING:	(*Eagerly*) Dae ye think sae, Sir Robert?
SIR ROBERT:	I am certain, not only because you intend to serve a cause she hath at heart, but because she must regard you now as sound in your religion, and therefore the most proper person, by your faith as by your birth and endowments, to succeed her on the Throne.
THE KING:	Ye think sae, Sir Robert?
MAITLAND:	Sir Robert hauds the best caird in the pack, yer Grace. He aye wins ye roun.
SIR ROBERT:	(*In protest*) My Lord!
THE KING:	Na na, Sir Robert, he's richt! Ye ken hou to play on my hopes o the succession!
SIR ROBERT:	Your hopes are brighter now, your Majesty, than the stars of heaven.
THE KING:	Awa wi ye. Flaittery wins nae favour frae me. Ye'll hae to show yer guid will in mair solid form. Hou sune dae ye think I can hae some siller?
SIR ROBERT:	As soon as the Queen my mistress hears of your resolve.
THE KING:	Then let her hear at ance. And I'll write to her mysell. Ye may tak yer letter.
SIR ROBERT:	Your Majesty, you are indeed merciful. Have you seen ought of my servant?
THE KING:	Ye deil, ye're wrigglin oot athegither! Yer servant's in the Tolbooth, and he'll bide

there the nou! I maun dae something to assert mysell! Gin it werena for the turn things hae taen Sir Robert, I wad be faur mair severe! Ye wad pack yer kist and mak for the Border! Ye bide on, ye understaun, for the sake o the guid will that maun exist atween mysell and yer royal mistress, but gin I fin ye up to ony mair o' yer intrigues I'll ask her to remove ye at ance!

SIR ROBERT: Your Majesty, I understand.

THE KING: Awa and think shame o yersell!

(Sir Robert *bows to the King, then to* Maitland, *then leaves. They watch him go*)

THE KING: I couldna be hard on him, for he's fired my hopes. Jock, I *will* pledge the bairn's praisents! They'll be safe nou. I can hae them back when his mistress pays up. Oho, but fortune's favoured me the day! There's naething in my wey! Aa that I hae wished for is promised at last! Bothwell on the scaffold, the Papists houndit doun, the Kirk in my pouer, England ahint me, and then, in the end, the dream o my life come true! It gars my pulse quicken! It gars my hairt loup! It gars my een fill wi tears! To think hou the twa pair countries hae focht and struggled. To think o the bluid they hae shed atween them, the touns they hae blackent wi fire, the bonnie green howes they hae laid waste. And then to think, as ae day it sall come to pass that I, Jamie Stewart, will ride to London, and the twa countries sall become ane.

(Mistress Edward *can be heard off calling* 'Nicoll! Nicoll! Come for yer supper!')

MAITLAND: (*Coming out of his trance and reaching for the bottle*) Ay, yer Grace, it's a solemn thocht. But the auld bitch isna deid yet.

(*He places the bottle before the* King. *The* King fills his glass)

THE KING: (*Raising his glass high*) Jock, here's to the day. May the mowdies[24] sune tickle her taes.

(Mistress Edward *appears at the door of the dining-room*)

MRS E: Yer Grace, the supper's ready.

(*The* King *and* Maitland *eye each other and drink the toast*)

CURTAIN

Robert McLellan

[24] moles

Auld Lang Syne

Should auld acquaintance be forgot,
   And never brought to mind?
Should auld acquaintance be forgot,
   And auld lang syne?

And surely ye'll be your pint-stowp!
   And surely I'll be mine!
And we'll tak a cup o' kindness yet,
   For auld lang syne!

We twa hae run about the braes,
   And pou'd the gowans fine;
But we've wander'd mony a weary fitt,
   Sin' auld lang syne.

We twa hae paidl'd in the burn,
   Frae morning sun till dine,
But seas between us braid hae roar'd
   Sin' auld lang syne.

[1]comrade

[2]deep draught of good will

And here's a hand, my trusty fiere![1]
   And gie's a hand o' thine!
And we'll take a right gude-willie waught,[2]
   For auld lang syne!

Robert Burns

Drug Treatment in Old Age Psychiatry

This book is to be returned on or before